CROQUET

Skills of the Game

CROQUET
Skills of the Game

BILL LAMB

THE CROWOOD PRESS 

First published in 1990 by
The Crowood Press Ltd
Ramsbury, Marlborough
Wiltshire SN8 2HR

www.crowood.com

Revised edition 2008

British Library Cataloguing-in-Publication Data
A catalogue record for this book is available from the British Library.

ISBN 978 1 86126 992 8

Dedication
For Mike, Dave and Chris and in memory of Rob.

Acknowledgements
I should like to acknowledge the assistance of all those players, too numerous to mention individually, who have contributed to my knowledge of the game. I thank also Dr G. A. Steigmann, who took most of the instructional photographs.

Line-drawings by Margaret Cree.

In this book the pronouns 'he', 'his' and 'him' have been used inclusively and are intended to refer to both men and women.

Typeset by Keyboard Services, Luton

Printed and bound in Spain by Graphy Cems

Contents

Introduction 1
Association Croquet 5
1 **Equipment** 8
The Croquet Court 8
2 **The Grip, Stance and Swing** 14
3 **Basic Technique** 21
Single-ball Shots 21
The Take-off 29
Straight Croquet Strokes 35
Split Croquet Strokes 43
4 **Applied Technique** 47
Hoop Approaches 47
Cannons 51
Peg-outs and Peels 58
Miscellaneous Shots 63
5 **Break Play** 71
6 **Tactics** 81
Openings 81
Leaves 86
The End-game 90
7 **Handicap Play** 95
8 **Advanced Play** 104
9 **Tournament Play** 109
10 **Winning Croquet** 112
Glossary 117
Index 121

Bill Lamb, a former university lecturer in physics, took up croquet in 1984 after a life-long interest in sport.

He served on the Croquet Association Council for eleven years from 1988 and was chairman for two years. He also chaired its coaching, laws, and handicap committees. During his time as coaching committee chairman, he contributed to and edited the CA coaching manual.

He is a past president of the European Croquet Federation and has coached in several European countries and in New Zealand.

Bill Lamb, current chairman of the Croquet Association's Coaching Committee, is one of the sport's most experienced coaches. He has the three essential attributes of a great coach: knowledge of his sport, being a top-class player; good teaching skills, acquired from his job as lecturer; and tremendous enthusiasm, which he transmits to his students. He has used these attributes to make croquet flourish in and around Yorkshire, once a croquet backwater. Through the medium of this book, which will help all croquet players from their initiation up to the A class, he now deservedly addresses a wider audience.

John McCullough
Former Coaching Committee Chairman

I have always found croquet an enjoyable game. To play it well requires good technique and discipline combined with a positive, relaxed mental attitude.

Over the past year, I have had several in-depth discussions with Bill Lamb on stroke production and how to play a good all-round game, and I have found his approach helpful to my own game. Because of this, I have no hesitation in recommending this book for all players, but especially for those who wish to improve. As technique, tactics and mental approach are all so important, even top players should use it to brush up on the finer points of their own game.

Joseph Hogan, World Champion, British and New Zealand Open Champion.

Introduction

This book assumes that the reader has some acquaintance with croquet and in this sense it is not a book for the absolute beginner; nor is it a book for those who are already expert. It is, instead, intended to help the vast majority of croquet players who would like to improve their play and increase their enjoyment of the game. I suspect that many readers will turn straight to Chapter 10 on how to win, but success will only come with sound technique, on which I lay great emphasis, and a sound knowledge of tactics.

I deal only with the game of Association Croquet, which is the most widespread form of competitive croquet and which makes more demands on technique than other versions.

Why Play Croquet?

Every sport has its adherents who enjoy and proclaim the advantages of their particular sport, but few can be played by such a wide range of people as croquet. The reason for this is that croquet is a game of pure skill; brute strength does not enter into the game and a powerfully built player has no physical advantage over one of more slender physique; nor does the game make any undue demands on stamina; a game may last as long as three or four hours but it is always played at walking pace. Moreover, croquet has an excellent handicap system which enables the beginner with perhaps only a season's experience to play against scratch players. As such the game can be played by young and old, male and female alike. Few sports can offer tournament play where women play on equal terms with men, where players in their early teens may play against those in their eighties. Many players have taken up the game when their days of playing a more active sport are over and exclamations of 'I wish I had taken it up years ago!' are commonly heard.

Croquet requires a feel or touch for single-ball shots which matches that of the bowls player, as well as the skill of a good snooker player in controlling the path of two balls in the croquet shot (from which the game derives its name). Indeed, croquet has much in common with snooker in its break-building but with the advantage of being played in the open air. Croquet is also a very gentlemanly game within the best meaning of that term; players act as their own referees during the course of a game, unless a particularly difficult shot is to be attempted. Such trust engenders a sense of sportsmanship and camaraderie which is far removed from the common conception of croquet as a vicious game.

All of these qualities enable croquet to claim with pride the title of 'queen of sports'.

A Brief History of the Game

Croquet is the generic name given to a number of games involving the use of hoops on a well-defined court, through which balls are struck with a mallet. The earliest record of such a game in the United Kingdom is 1851, although it is thought that the idea was imported from Ireland, where the game may have been played as early as the 1830s. By

Fig 1 The 1990 Great Britain Test Team.

1862 Jaques & Son, a firm which is still trading today under the name of John Jaques & Son Ltd., published a price-list for equipment referring to prize medals. The game rapidly became popular amongst the leisured and well-to-do.

In 1867 the first known tournament was held at Evesham and in the following year the All-England Croquet Club was formed. The game flourished until the invention of *Sphairistike*, soon to become known as lawn tennis, when many croquet lawns were converted to tennis courts. Croquet then went into decline until the 1890s, when tournament play was resumed and its popularity increased steadily until the outbreak of the First World War. The United All-England Croquet Association was formed in 1896 and changed its name to the Croquet Association in 1900.

International croquet was born in 1925 with the first Test match between England and Australia. These two countries were soon joined by New Zealand and the aim of most top-class players is to represent their country in this triangular series of matches, which takes place every three years.

The Second World War almost brought croquet to a stop and its recovery afterwards was a slow affair – until the early 1960s, when an influx of new and younger players started an increase in popularity.

The principal form of the game played nowadays is known officially as Association Croquet, to distinguish it from other forms of the game, although the shorter term croquet is generally used.

The Croquet Association

Croquet is controlled today by the Croquet Association, membership of which is open to individual players as well as clubs. The Croquet Association, or CA as it is usually known, is strictly speaking responsible for croquet in England only, although its expertise is generally recognised by the countries of the United Kingdom, which also have their own associations.

The CA also organises the calendar of tournaments and championships held throughout England and appoints official tournament managers, referees and handicappers. A magazine, *Croquet*, is published every two months.

England is divided into regions, each of which has a development officer and a coaching officer, who arrange coaching for beginners and assist with the formation of new clubs. Weekend coaching courses for players, from improvers to experts, are arranged during the playing season on a national basis.

The CA was a founder member and host to the inaugural meeting of the World Croquet Federation (WCF) held immediately before the first World Croquet Championship at the Hurlingham Club in July 1989. The WCF has assumed responsibility for the laws of the game, although the CA still plays a leading role.

Fig 2 A weekend advanced coaching course at Bowdon.

Fig 3 The World Championships at the Hurlingham Club.

Fig 4 Joseph Hogan (NZ), winner of the Inaugural World Championship, receives the Wimbledon Cup.

Getting Started

Association Croquet is not an easy game for the uninitiated to play. Indeed, one of the game's attractions is the variety of strokes required and the tactical manoeuvres necessary to pick up and play a break.

Undoubtedly, the best way for beginners, or even for those who may have played some croquet in their gardens, to make progress is to join one of the courses arranged by a regional coaching officer in conjunction with a croquet club. Then the player will have the benefit of instruction from a qualified CA coach, as well as temporary membership of the club, for a course fee of only a few pounds. Each course consists of five or six lessons usually at the rate of one per week, each lesson lasting one-and-a-half to two hours.

During the early part of the course there will be an introduction to some of the easier games of croquet, such as golf croquet, to give players the chance to enjoy a little friendly competition amongst themselves. All equipment will be provided so that there is no outlay required apart from the course fee. The only stipulation will be that players must wear flat-soled shoes whilst on the croquet lawn in order not to damage the turf. As croquet is a summer sport, these organised courses are usually held in May or June, giving the rest of the season to those who subsequently decide to take up the game. In many clubs the course fee can be offset against the first year's subscription.

As an alternative, the CA organises a number of residential summer schools taking advantage of the cheap accommodation which is available in universities and private schools during the summer vacation. These courses are more intensive, last four or five days and offer the relaxation of a good holiday. For more information on summer schools or where to find the nearest croquet club just write, preferably enclosing an SAE, to:

The Croquet Association
c/o Cheltenham Croquet Club
Old Bath Road
Cheltenham GL53 7DF
www.croquet.org.uk

ASSOCIATION CROQUET

The Object of the Game

The game is, in effect, a race between two players. One player plays with the red and yellow balls, the other player with the blue and black. Each player is trying to play each of his balls through the hoops in the correct sequence and against the peg before his opponent can do likewise. Each time a player runs a hoop with one of his balls he scores a point. As the six hoops are run by a player's two balls in both directions, a full game consists of twenty-six points, i.e. twenty-four hoop points and two peg points. A ball can only score a peg point if it has already scored twelve hoop points, in which case it is known as a rover. A rover can cause any other rover to score a peg point. A ball which scores a peg point is said to be pegged out and is removed from the game.

The Play of the Game

At the start of the game the balls are played successively into the court from either of the two baulk-lines, although hoop points and roquets (hitting another ball) may be made before all of the balls are on the court.

The players take turns. At the start of his turn the player chooses which ball he wishes to play with. The ball chosen is

Fig 5 Keith Aiton correctly replaces the ball on the yard-line with his back to the court.

known as the striker's ball for the duration of the turn and is the only ball he may hit with his mallet; his other ball is known as the partner ball. Each time the player makes a successful stroke he becomes entitled to play one further stroke. A successful stroke is one in which the striker's ball scores a hoop point by running its next hoop in order or makes a roquet by hitting another ball. A ball which makes a roquet becomes a 'ball in hand'. It is picked up and placed in contact with the ball which has just been roqueted in order to play a croquet stroke. The croquet stroke is played by hitting the striker's ball in such a way as to cause both balls to move and is unique, amongst ball games, to croquet. The croqueted ball may not be sent off the court in a successful croquet stroke; nor may the striker's ball, unless it has roqueted another ball in the same croquet stroke.

The striker's ball may roquet each of the other three balls (and therefore take croquet from them) but once a ball has been roqueted, it may not be roqueted again in that turn until the striker's ball has scored its next hoop point. As soon as the striker's ball has scored a hoop point in a turn, it once again becomes entitled to roquet each of the other three balls.

A single turn progresses through a series of successful strokes, in which either a hoop point is scored, a roquet is made or a lawful croquet stroke is played. After a hoop point has been scored or a lawful croquet stroke has been played, the next stroke is known as a continuation stroke. The turn comes to an end when a continuation stroke fails to score a hoop point or make a roquet, or when an unlawful croquet stroke is played.

During a turn any ball played off the court is replaced on the yard-line; any ball other than the striker's ball played into the yard-line area is also replaced on the yard-line. At the end of a turn all balls off the court or in the yard-line area are replaced on the yard-lines.

Doubles Play

Each player in the pair has his own colour ball and may play with that ball only. The pairs take turns and at the start of the turn either player in the pair may play the turn. Otherwise, the laws are as for singles play.

1 Equipment

THE CROQUET COURT *(Fig 6)*

A full-size croquet court measures 35 × 28yd (32 × 25.6m) and is laid out as seen in Fig 6. Note that the module of length is 7yd (6.4m). A small court can be set out by reducing this basic module as circumstances require, thus retaining the relative proportions of the full-size court. The hoops are run in the order and direction indicated and are called 1 to 6 on the outward half and 1-back to 4-back plus penult and rover for the inward half.

In Fig 6 the dotted lines are the imaginary yard-lines on which balls that are struck out of the playing area are replaced. This yard is conveniently measured by the player with the use of his mallet, so avoiding the need to have them permanently marked out. The A and B baulk-lines are the parts of the yard-lines from which balls may be played into court.

For convenience the boundaries are named by the points of the compass and this is reflected when describing positions. The south boundary is always the shorter boundary adjacent to hoop 1 regardless of the geographical orientation of the court. The corners are numbered 1 to 4 according to the nearest hoop, and in tournament play their positions are indicated by coloured flags. Small white pegs indicate the ends of the yard-lines.

Key to the Diagrams

S or ●	Striker's ball
O	Other Balls
C	Ball to be croqueted
T	Third ball
R	Red
Y	Yellow
Bu	Blue
Bk	Black
R1,2,3 etc	Sequential positions of the red ball. Similar notation for the other colours

The Lawn

A croquet court can be laid out on any lawn which is reasonably flat and level provided that the grass is short enough for the balls to roll smoothly without rising or flying. If the lawn is not level, the path of the balls will curve if they roll across the slope and different strength shots will be required to play up and down the slope. Whilst this may add to the fun of garden croquet, it is hardly conducive to serious play. Similarly, if the lawn is bumpy, firmly struck shots will bounce and jump around the lawn making it extremely difficult to play with precision. However, perfectly flat and level croquet lawns are rare and players accept the contours of most club lawns.

In addition, a good lawn which will test the skills of the most expert players should be

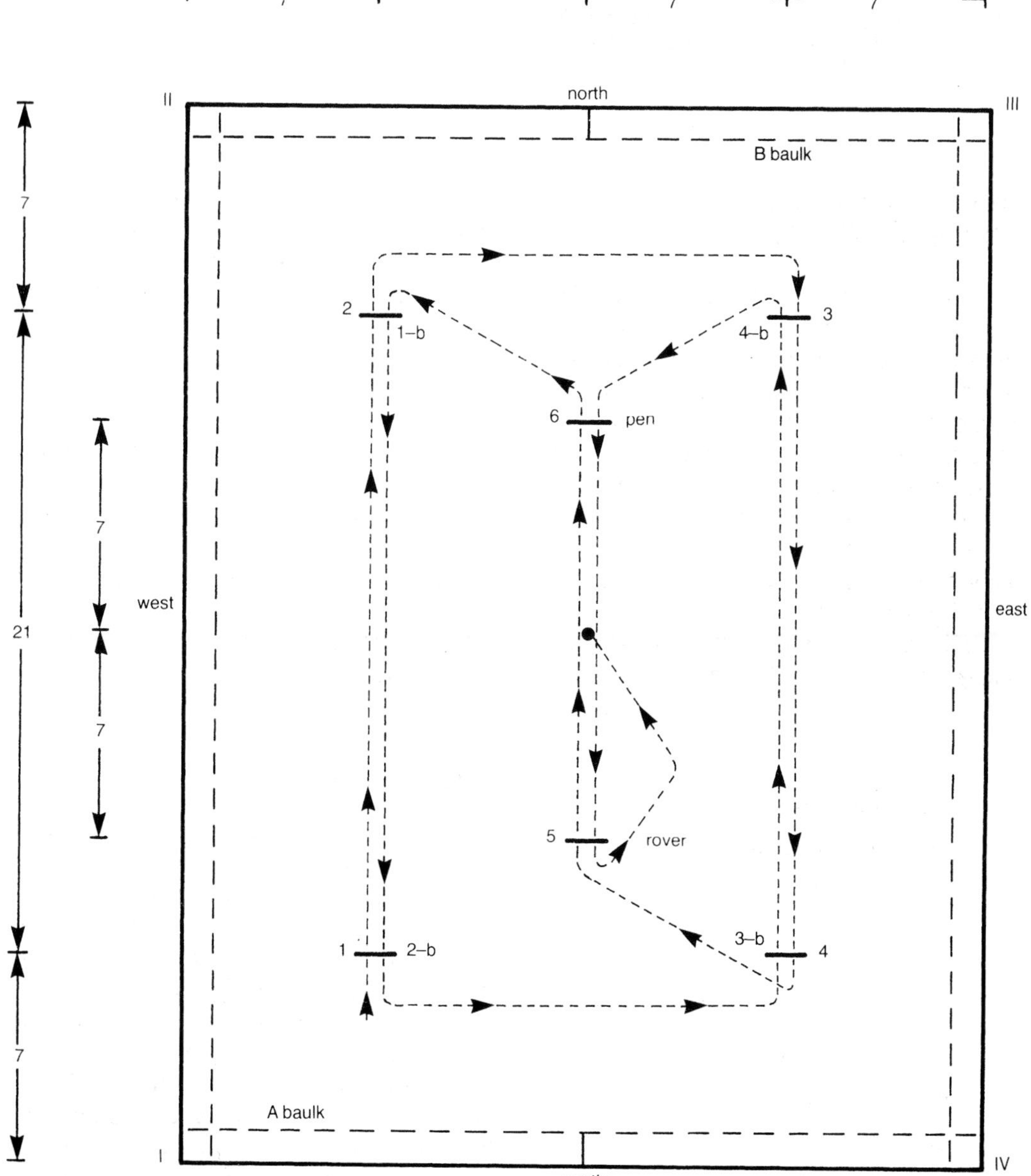

Fig 6 Court layout. (All measurements in yards.)

firm and fast. This means that the lawn should not be watered except in the dryest conditions and the grass should not be over-fertilised. The grass should be cut as short as is practicable without scalping the lawn. Alas, in England the average rainfall is

Fig 7 Championship hoop and ball: the gap should be not more than one-eighth of an inch nor less than one-sixteenth.

too high for firm, fast lawns to be encountered, except during the occasional hot, dry summer, and easy-paced lawns tend to flatter the weaker players.

Hoops *(Figs 7 and 8)*

Hoops should be of championship standard, made of cast iron with solid 'carrots', which will be firm and rigid when placed in the court. The flimsier type of hoop made of bent wire will be too yielding when struck by a ball, making it far too easy to run hoops from difficult positions. A core of earth should be removed for each carrot before driving the hoops into the court, otherwise the earth will rise around the hoop leading to a 'hoop on a hill'.

The setting of the hoops may depend upon the standard of play expected. For normal tournament play the internal width of the hoop is set to $3\frac{3}{4}$in (9.5cm), giving a gap between hoop and ball of $\frac{1}{8}$in (3mm). This gap is reduced to $\frac{1}{16}$ (1.5mm) for open championships and international events. Many clubs with predominantly high handicap or older players have more generous hoop settings to avoid making the game too difficult. However, careless or inaccurate play, particularly around the hoops, should be penalised; if the hoops are too generous, the game becomes too easy for the expert players.

The Winning Peg

The peg is a round wooden stake, usually with a tapered end to assist driving it into the ground, and stands 18 in (45cm) clear. The top contains a removable, narrow extension piece to hold clips. The bottom of the peg should be painted white to a height 6in (15cm) from the ground. This is an item of equipment which can easily be manufactured at home for the sake of economy.

Clips

A set of four metal or plastic clips, painted to match the colours of the balls, is used to indicate the score to the players. At the end of each scoring turn the position of the clips is adjusted to show the next hoop for each ball, with the clip placed on the top of the hoop on the outward half and on the side for the inward half. Plastic 'jumbo' clothes-pegs make a good cheap substitute.

Fig 8 Court equipment.

Balls

Croquet balls weigh 16oz (454g) and have a nominal diameter of 3⅝in (9.2cm). Formerly, croquet balls were made with a composition core surrounded by a hard plastic skin. However, such balls were time-consuming to make and therefore expensive. Moreover, they were not very durable. The development of a solid plastic ball that is easier and cheaper to produce proved difficult initially. The problem was to find a material with the right density to provide a ball with the correct dimensions and weight, and at the same time with an elasticity to make it play like a traditional croquet ball. If the ball is too elastic, the rush stroke is easier to play but, conversely, it is much harder to play the roll stroke. To encourage development, the range of permitted elasticity was quite large, which resulted in balls with widely differing playing characteristics. However, the problem has been solved and solid plastic balls are now usually used. All manufacturers must submit balls for testing and approval, which is carried out by the CA on behalf of the WCF.

If you play as a member of a croquet club, the balls will be provided. If you wish to buy a set of balls for your own use, approved balls can be obtained from the CA.

Mallets *(Fig 9)*

The mallet is the most personal piece of croquet equipment and beginners would be well advised to try as many club mallets of different types as possible before making their choice. A mallet can weigh between

Fig 9 A selection of mallets.

2lb 8oz (1kg) and 4lb (1.8kg) (most players prefer a weight near 3lb (1.4kg)) with a shaft length of between 30 and 40in (75 and 100cm), according to the height of the player and the style of play.

Traditionally, the mallet head was made of lignum vitae to withstand the strain of constantly hitting croquet balls. However, lignum vitae is very expensive and sometimes difficult to obtain. Other hardwoods are not dense enough to produce a mallet heavier than 3lb (1.4kg) and indeed they wear down more quickly. The shaft was made of ash or hickory, sometimes split at the lower end with a cane insert glued in.

Nowadays, mallet heads are made from a variety of materials such as nylon, permali (an impregnated and laminated wood) or hardwood with nylon or tufnel end faces – as well as the traditional lignum vitae. Mallet heads made out of lighter woods usually incorporate brass weights to bring them up to the desired weight. Aluminium and fibreglass or carbon fibre shafts have also become popular and are stronger than hickory. Fibreglass, in particular, is immensely strong and flexible. Carbon fibre is stiffer and extremely light, which permits the balance of the mallet to be lower down the shaft. There are, however, drawbacks with these modern materials in that they do not possess such good damping factors as wood and shaft vibration can cause or aggravate problems with wrist or elbow tendons. If a mallet with a wooden shaft is chosen, care should be taken that the grain is straight down the shaft and is not twisted.

Lignum vitae is an oily wood which will dry out and possibly open up cracks if exposed to high temperatures. For this reason it is not wise to leave such a mallet in a car on a hot day. The head should also be oiled with teak oil or a good-quality wood oil at the end of the season. If a mallet with a laminated head is used frequently in wet conditions, there is a tendency for the head to split along a lamination. These mallets should be kept well varnished to keep out water. If the mallet does split, it can easily be repaired by opening up the split with a wedge, squeezing in a good modern wood adhesive (such as Evostick Resin W) and clamping the head tight in a vice overnight.

Clothing

Flat-soled shoes are necessary for croquet and it is sensible to make sure that they are comfortable as players may be on their feet for most of the day. Modern sports shoes with nylon-mesh uppers allow the feet to breathe on the warmest days and are well cushioned but they are not waterproof; leather or synthetic uppers are an improvement but will not withstand very wet conditions, whereas shoes which are completely waterproof are not very kind to the feet. Perhaps the best solution for tournament play is to keep a change of shoes and socks handy.

In most clubs there is no stipulation to wear whites during ordinary play but the general entry conditions for a tournament require clothing to be predominantly white. White or cream flannels, or shorts according to the weather, with a white sports shirt and sweater are usual for men. Women usually wear slacks or a divided or short skirt.

As tournaments do not come to a stop when it rains, a good set of waterproofs is necessary. The type which allow perspiration to permeate the fabric but keep rain out are the most comfortable; such a set with the CA logo can be obtained from the CA at an advantageous price.

2 The Grip, Stance and Swing

In the British Isles croquet is a minority sport with no professional coaching. No basic grip, stance or swing has evolved which can be taught to all beginners, unlike the situation in a sport such as golf. Beginners have usually been left to imitate the better players in their club. Even today coaching courses spend little time on these aspects of the game; it is generally felt better, and perhaps rightly so in view of the complicated nature of croquet, to press on and teach beginners the elements of the game in the limited time available. Nevertheless, those who wish to make progress in the game would do well to study the general principles of body mechanics involved in hitting a stationary ball.

There are two different styles in croquet. In the side style the mallet is swung by the

Fig 10(a) The standard grip, hands separated: front view.

Fig 10(b) Side view.

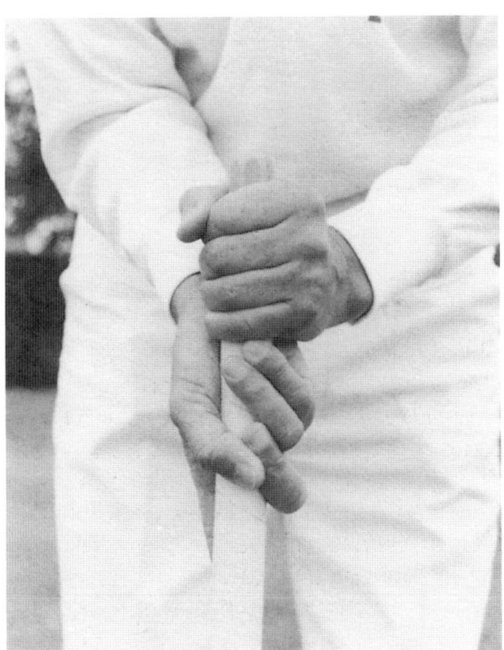

Fig 11(a) The standard grip, hands together: front view.

Fig 11(b) Side view.

side of the body allowing a swing which is not impeded by the body itself. In the centre style the mallet is swung between the legs, permitting the head to be more naturally over the ball. The side style was fashionable many years ago, particularly amongst the ladies whose long skirts prevented them from using the centre style, but few players use it today.

The secret of accurate hitting lies in the swing, which is itself conditioned by the grip and stance.

The Grip

There are three basic ways to hold a croquet mallet; standard, Irish and Solomon.

The Standard Grip (Figs 10 and 11)

With the standard grip the mallet is held with the knuckles of the upper hand and the palm of the lower hand facing forward. Beginners usually choose this grip with the hands held well apart, but are advised to try to bring the hands closer together when they become used to swinging what is, initially, a rather unwieldy object. When the hands are separated, the lower hand provides most of the power and the upper hand the pivot or guidance.

The Irish Grip (Fig 12)

The Irish grip usually has the hands lower down the shaft of the mallet with the palms of the hands facing forward or to the side. Irish grippers often choose a mallet with a shorter shaft. This grip has the advantage of being more symmetrical, with the hands sharing the work, and can be a very accurate grip, particularly on short shots. However, the Irish grip can put a great deal of strain on the wrists and beginners often have difficulty hitting the ball hard enough.

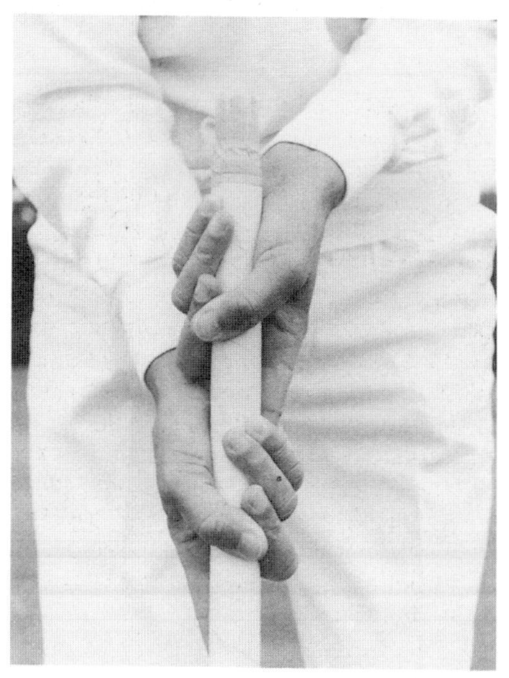

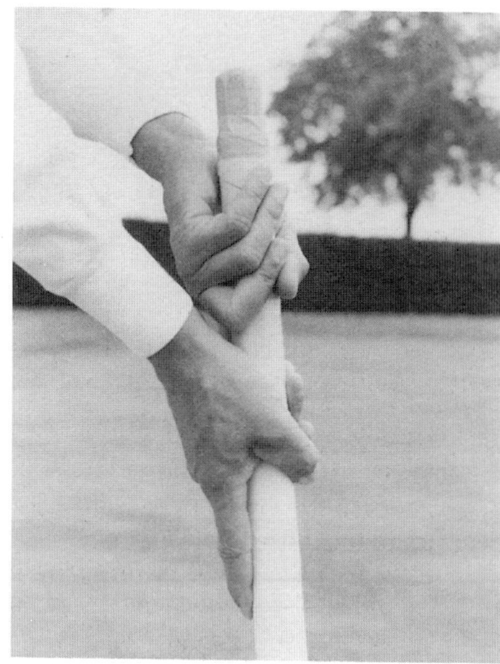

Fig 12(a) The Irish grip front view. *(b) Side view.*

Fig 13(a) The Solomon grip: front view. *(b) Side view.*

The Solomon Grip (Fig 13)

In contrast to the Irish grip, with the Solomon grip the hands are at the top of the mallet with both knuckles facing forward. At first, this grip can seem very awkward, as the hands are a long way from the mallet head, but it has the advantage that the hands are working together and permit a long back swing. It is, therefore, a very powerful grip.

The Stance

The natural pivot points for the swing are the shoulders and, whatever stance you adopt, the shoulders should be square to the line of aim. If this is not achieved, the shoulder joints will be asymmetrical and the swing will be at an angle to the shoulders. It is equally important for the development of a straight swing that the shoulders are horizontal. Otherwise, the natural line of the swing will be an arc which comes inside the straight line on both the back swing and the follow-through. Shoulder alignment is the commonest error made by erratic players.

If you choose to play side style, the stance and grip will be forced upon you. Your grip will have to be the standard grip and the fact that the ball and mallet are to your side whilst you are trying to get your head over the ball will force you to put most of your weight on one leg, with the other to the side and behind to provide balance.

If you are right-handed, your weight should be on your right foot, which should point in the direction of your aim. The left forearm should be approximately horizontal (for this reason side-style players usually require a mallet with a long shaft) and the hips and shoulders square to the direction of aim.

Centre-style players should try to adopt a stance which is as symmetric as possible, with the feet side by side, provided that this does not cause any problems with balance. The feet should point in the direction of your aim and be reasonably close together with the weight distributed equally. However, if you have difficulty keeping your balance without rocking excessively during the swing or if you play the standard grip with the hands well separated, you may have to adopt a stance with one foot pulled back. Take care, however, that in so doing the corresponding hip and shoulder are not also pulled back. At the same time try to keep the weight distributed equally between the feet; if you place more weight on your front foot, there will be a tendency to lean to that side.

The Swing

General Principles

In theory, all that is required in order to hit a ball accurately is to strike the ball with the end-face square to the intended direction of travel; in practice, this turns out to be difficult to achieve. The simpler and straighter the swing, the more likely it is that the desired result will be achieved; the more complicated the swing, the more you will have to rely on timing to bring the mallet head back into line. Players who have complicated swings are apt to spray the ball around when their timing goes astray. Above all else, the swing should be smooth and seemingly effortless.

The mallet should feel as though it is a natural extension of the arms and hands and should be moving in sympathy with them at all times. The simplest, straightest swing is pendulum-like in its motion and there should be no attempt to force the mallet, particularly when hitting hard. The mallet is quite heavy enough to deal with the most powerful shots required and should be permitted to do the work.

The swing comes principally from the shoulders and is mainly a movement of the mallet and arms. The wrists should be allowed to cock naturally with the motion of the mallet, and the transition from back swing to forward swing should be smooth, leading to a firm hit and natural follow-through.

Ideally, the head and body should be perfectly still, but this can lead to a rather stiff action with loss of sensitivity on touch shots. Most players prefer to allow a little body movement but the position of the head should not change.

The Take-away

It is not easy to start the mallet moving smoothly; it is, after all, a fairly heavy object at rest. Start the take-away slowly and as smoothly as possible by drawing the arms back. If you find that the mallet moves sideways or twists, slide the mallet back along the grass in the initial movement. Alternatively, try pulling back gently with the arms without moving the head of the mallet along the ground, and then lift the mallet. The head will then fall back under its own weight. Be careful not to exaggerate this initial movement, for it can lead to the movement of the arms and mallet getting out of synchronism.

Fig 14 The back swing.

The Back Swing (Fig 14)

The mallet should then be accelerated steadily back from the take-away to a point approximately half-way through the back swing. The wrists will cock naturally as the arm movement becomes limited. Let the mallet decelerate smoothly to the top of the back swing. This is perhaps the most crucial point of the whole swing. Stand behind any player with a crooked swing and you will see the mallet twist at the top of the back swing, usually because the player is in too much of a hurry to hit the ball. If the hands start to move forwards whilst the mallet head is moving backwards, the twist is almost inevitable. Hands and mallet should stop moving simultaneously. Ask someone to stand behind you to check whether you have an excessive twist at the top of your back swing. If you do, make a conscious effort to pause at the top of the back swing.

The Forward Swing

From the top of the back swing the mallet and arms will accelerate steadily through to the point of impact. Try to follow the natural rhythm of the swing and do not force this acceleration. If you find it difficult to feel this

Fig 15 The impact.

Fig 16 The follow-through.

rhythm, try holding the mallet at your side with your top hand only and start it swinging gently backwards and forwards like a pendulum.

The Impact and Follow-through (Figs 15 and 16)

It is important not to quit on the shot before the ball is struck and to continue hitting through the shot and afterwards into the follow-through. The arms should extend naturally if you do this. If you fail to hit through the ball, there is a danger that you will relax your grip too early and the mallet will twist, unless you hit the ball dead in the centre of the mallet. The follow-through is regarded as essential in all sports involving hitting, although all would agree that the follow-through cannot influence the ball once it has departed. The importance of the follow-through lies more in its influence in keeping the mallet on line during impact.

Continuous Swinging

Some players, and particularly in recent years some younger players, tend to swing the mallet backwards and forwards above the ball until the aim and rhythm of the swing feel right. They then duck down from the waist to strike the ball on the final swing. This can be a useful method to try if you are experiencing a loss of form in shooting, due to losing the rhythm of the swing.

Of course, it is impossible to concentrate on all of these points whilst actually hitting a ball. In fact, it would be quite counter-productive, for the swing, once acquired, should be subconscious. But it is worthwhile trying to acquire a smooth, graceful swing. You can still be a good player and a good shot without it, but it is unlikely that you will be consistently good.

Above all, you should feel comfortable with your grip, stance and swing. If you are not comfortable, there is the danger that the repetitive movements of swinging the mallet in play or practice can lead to repetitive strain injury (RSI). Players who use the Irish grip with the hands held high are particularly prone to RSI.

3 Basic Technique

SINGLE-BALL SHOTS

The Roquet *(Figs 17 and 18)*

Before taking up your stance to shoot at a target ball, stand back a few yards on the line joining the two balls, then approach the ball you are going to strike with the mallet by walking along this line whilst looking at the target ball. This exercise, known as stalking the ball, will help to get the body and feet set up properly for the stance and is an essential prerequisite for all single-ball shots. If, having arrived at the ball, you feel that something is not quite right, resist the temptation to try to adjust the position of your feet or the direction of your aim; instead, walk back and start the process over again. You may find it helpful to raise or swing your mallet forwards over the ball, to confirm that your aim at the target ball is accurate.

Finally, place your mallet behind the ball, concentrate your gaze on the ball, relax by taking in one deep breath, breathe out and hold this position, then swing. The reason for

Fig 17 Stalk the ball along the line.

Fig 18 The roquet: Chris Clarke.

shooting whilst holding the exhaled state is to avoid the shoulder movement which occurs during normal breathing. It does not matter whether you look at the back, centre or front of the ball you are striking, as long as you concentrate on this spot throughout the swing. Normal eye and muscle co-ordination is extremely well developed in most people and if you move your eyes during the swing, the mallet will certainly follow.

Beware of looking up too quickly in your anxiety to see whether you have hit or missed! It can cause the head to come up before the ball has been struck and lead to a topped or mishit shot. Equally, it is not necessary to continue to stare at the spot at your feet long after the ball has gone. I have seen several instances where, by doing this, a player has not realised that a roquet has just been nicked. Your opponent may not realise it either, if he is sitting thirty yards away. Rather, let your head come up naturally as part of the follow-through.

Practice Exercises (Figs 19–21)

Some people have an enviable ability to hit straight; the rest of us must practise until the swing is as automatic as, say, walking. You should not have to think about it; even more, you should never worry about it. To build up your confidence, you should make certain that your practice is successful and that your preparation for each practice shot is as careful as if it were a shot in a match. Loosen up a little by hitting a ball around for a couple of minutes before you start practising in earnest.

If you do not have a suitable back-stop such as a boundary board, you can use a fixed target ball. This can be constructed by drilling an old ball through the centre with a ⅜in or ½in drill and gluing a 12in (30cm) piece of metal rod into it. The protruding end

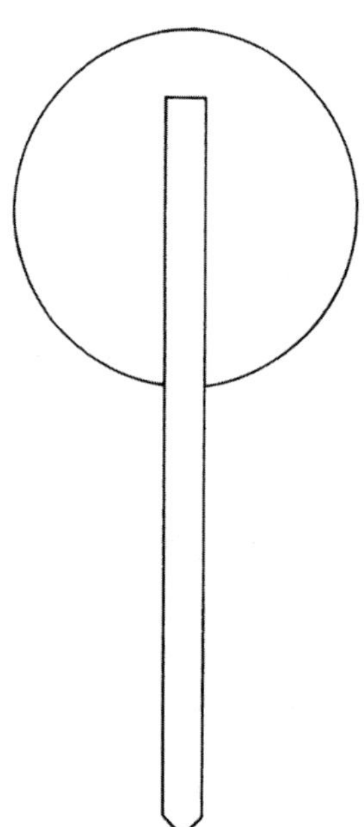

Fig 19 Practice target ball.

Fig 20 A spiked, practice target ball.

can be sharpened and pushed into the ground to give a target which is not displaced when hit.

Take a couple of sets of balls and start your practice by shooting at the target ball over a short distance so that you are certain to hit it. You will have to establish this distance by experiment, the criterion being that you must hit with eight successive shots. Increase the distance between the balls gradually by about a yard after each set of eight shots and find the distance at which you can hit with seven shots out of eight. Repeat to find the distance at which you hit six out of eight. These distances can be used as bench-marks for subsequent practice.

Always start your roquet practice sessions at the shortest of the three distances and work upwards. Do not permit yourself to proceed to the next bench-mark until you have been successful with the current one. When you have achieved the longest bench-mark successfully, come back down via the intermediate bench-mark to the shortest.

The whole exercise will only take ten to fifteen minutes and, if you do not make any mistakes, you will have had forty shots and will have been successful with at least thirty-six. These are the bread and butter distances in croquet and it is more important in match play not to miss these distances than to hit occasional long shots. Not only will you be able to increase your bench-marks as your shooting improves, but you will also build up a mental attitude that you expect to hit these roquets. Moreover, your shooting at longer distances will automatically improve as your accuracy at the shorter shots improves.

It is very easy to get your alignment slightly out, even after stalking the ball. Try the following check, which requires only four skewers or tent pegs and a few yards of string. Stretch two lengths of string between the skewers so that you have two parallel lines separated by the width of your normal stance. Place the target centrally between the lines at the far end and stalk the ball. Your feet should end up in position on the lines, pointing along them.

Fig 21 Target practice: the lines help to get the feet set up correctly.

Hoop Running *(Figs 22–6)*

The same general principles of preparation and swing apply to hoop-running as to making a roquet. The ball and hoop should be properly stalked, lining up the centre of the ball with the centre of the hoop for straight hoop shots. If the hoop is angled, i.e. you are not straight in front of it, the lining-up procedure is rather different. Here the aim should be such that the ball just

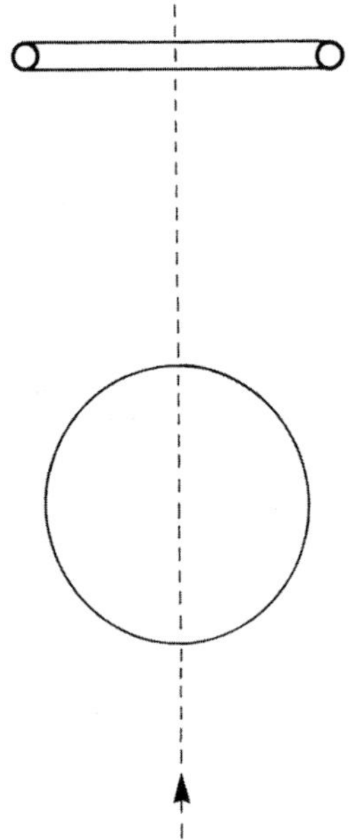

Fig 22 Straight hoop running.

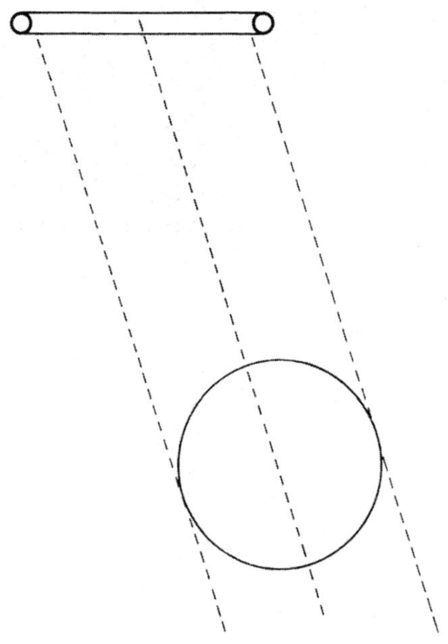

Fig 23 Angled hoop running.

Fig 24 A nicely controlled hoop. (Note David Openshaw's follow-through.)

misses the near wire. Provided that the angle is not too severe, the ball will be deflected by the far wire through the hoop. The natural top-spin of the ball caused by its rolling action will help this process. If it does strike the near wire, it will be deflected away from the hoop and fail to run it.

It is sometimes claimed that a good follow-through will help to put forward spin on the ball, thus helping it through the hoop if it should catch a side-wire. In fact, the longer the mallet is in contact with ball, the more the onset of rolling is delayed, because of the friction between them. Nevertheless, the follow-through is still important in keeping the swing on line. Provided that the ball maintains contact with the ground and is not struck too hard, it will be rolling fully by the time it has travelled a few inches. Any attempt to modify either the swing by lifting the mallet on contact or the stance to

Fig 25 Mark Avery.

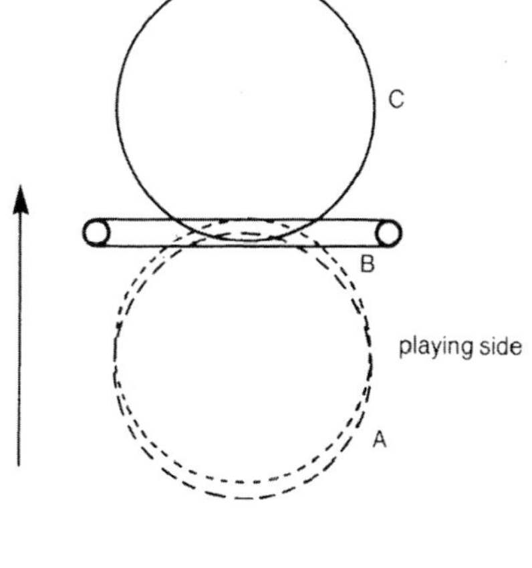

Fig 26 A has not started to run the hoop; B has started to run the hoop; C has completed the running of the hoop.

hit the ball after the bottom of the swing in order to induce more top-spin is unnecessary.

Most players make the mistake of running hoops too hard, particularly if they are angled. There is an understandable fear that the ball may stick in the hoop and they try to compensate by hitting harder than is necessary. This can be counter-productive in two ways: firstly, the harder you hit, the more likely the swing is to be inaccurate; secondly, you are more likely to lift the ball off the ground and prevent it rolling fully by the time it reaches the hoop. Concentrate instead on swinging smoothly and gently – it will pay dividends.

Remember that a ball does not have to pass completely through a hoop in order to run it. A ball starts to run a hoop as soon as its front meets the plane defined by the edges of the wires on the non-playing side. It completes the running of the hoop when its back passes the plane defined by the edges of the wires on the playing side. It is common practice to test the latter by sliding the mallet down the playing side of the hoop to see if contact is made with the ball. In tournament play this must not be done by the player, even to decide whether to call a referee.

One of the hallmarks of expert play is controlled hoop running. If the ball is a few inches straight in front of the hoop, try to run it through exactly to reach a predetermined point on the other side without touching either wire. The better your swing, the further away from the hoop you can try for control.

Practice Exercises

Concentrate your hoop-running practice on the shorter distances at first. There is very little to be gained by blasting away at hoops from several yards. Start with a set of balls and place one 6in (15cm) straight in front of the hoop and hit it through the hoop without touching the wires a distance of about 1yd (91cm). Repeat the exercise from the same distance but this time send the ball about 18in (45cm) through the hoop.

Move back to 1ft (30cm), then 2ft (60cm) and finally 1yd (91cm) from the hoop. From 1ft (30cm) you should still be able to run the hoop without touching the wires but at the longer distances it is likely that you will clip one of them. Strike the ball with sufficient force to send it no more than 1yd (91cm) through the hoop. In this way you will acquire the confidence to run hoops gently.

Fig 27 The rush: Colin Irwin.

Now place a ball 6in (15cm) in front of a hoop and try to hit it through the hoop so it goes no more than 6in (15cm) on the other side. Then turn round and run the hoop back again in the same manner. At first, you will probably find that you hit the ball too hard. See how many times you can run the hoop from alternate sides without the ball either sticking in the hoop or going through by more than 1ft (30cm).

Try angled hoops from 1ft (30cm) in front and 3in (7.5cm) to the side. You will have to hit harder than for a straight hoop because now you intend to hit the far wire and deflect the ball through the hoop, but not so hard that you are trying to 'bully' the ball through the hoop. Again the ball should run through no more than 1yd (91cm). Increase the distance, but not the angle, in stages until you are 1yd (91cm) away.

In these exercises keep your swing as smooth as possible with a good follow-through and avoid any tendency to jab at the ball. It is a good idea to set up a practice hoop just off the lawn to avoid creating 'rabbit runs' in the hoops on the lawn. If this is not possible, avoid practising hoop running at the same hoop.

The Rush *(Fig 27)*

The difference between the rush and the roquet is that with the roquet you are usually content to hit the target ball, whereas with the rush you are trying to knock the target ball to a chosen spot. Once you have a consistent swing the rush is one of the easiest and most valuable shots to play, yet most high-bisquers find it rather daunting. The general principles are the same as with the other single-ball shots. Stalk the ball carefully, relax, swing and follow through.

The Straight Rush

With the straight rush you are trying to hit the target ball straight along the extension of the line joining the centres of the balls as they lie. Your line of aim is therefore exactly the same as it would be for a roquet.

You may find that your ball has an annoying tendency to hit the target ball above centre and climb up the back of it, so failing to transfer sufficient momentum. The most likely cause is that you are becoming distracted by the target ball because it is within your peripheral vision. If, at any time during the swing you start to look towards the target ball, there will be a tendency for your weight to come too far forwards on the downswing, so that you strike the ball before the mallet is at the bottom of the swing, squeezing the ball between the mallet and turf. The ball will then jump out of the 'V' instead of rolling along the ground.

The advice sometimes given is to allow for this effect by standing back a few inches. However, if you stand too far back, you may strike the ball after the low point of the swing, thus hitting it upwards and producing a result equivalent to that which you are trying to avoid. It is far better to correct an error than to make allowance for it. Keep your normal stance and ignore the target ball!

The Cut Rush (Figs 28 and 29)

Often you will find in play that you want to rush a ball to the left or right, i.e. you want to cut the rush. Snooker or billiard players will recognise the principle immediately; the line of aim should be that which brings the two balls into contact so that the extension of the line between their centres is in the direction you want the target ball to go. To find this line of aim imagine that there is a ball in contact with the ball to be roqueted in the correct

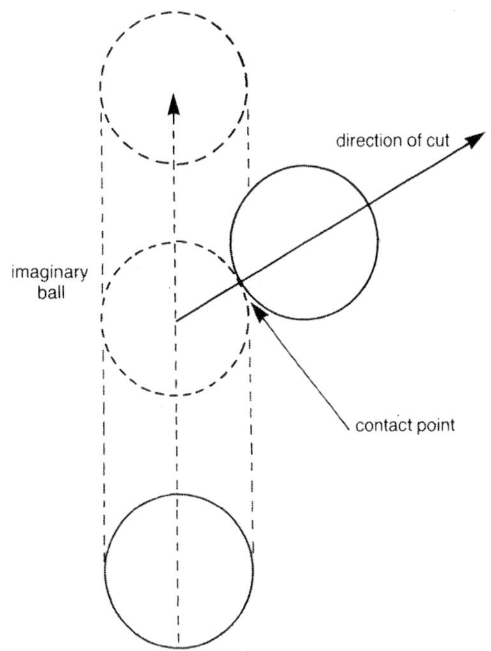

Fig 28 Cut rush.

Fig 29 Mark Saurin prepares for the cut rush.

position and make this imaginary ball your target. You may even find it useful to point to the centre of the imaginary ball to define more precisely the spot on the grass at which you are aiming.

You will have to hit the cut rush harder than the straight rush in order to make the rushed ball travel the same distance. With the straight rush your ball will lose nearly all its momentum on impact, whereas with the cut rush your ball with be deflected and maintain some of its momentum. Of course, in trying to hit harder there is a danger that you may completely miss the ball to be rushed. Also, the closer you are to the ball to be rushed, the more it must be cut in order to rush it in the right direction. These two points make the cut rush much more difficult to execute, so do not be too ambitious. You may decide to try a straight rush when the balls are separated by a couple of yards or so, but the cut rush should only be attempted at distances much less than this.

Fig 30 The dolly rush: Robert Fulford.

Although a complete miss is more frustrating and more damaging in terms of the loss of the innings during a game, the more common mistake is to fail to cut the rush sufficiently. The mistake once again is to look towards the ball to be rushed, so dragging the swing over in that direction. Once you have selected your line of aim, ignore everything else until you have struck your ball and are into the follow-through. If you wear a cap or hat whilst playing and have problems with the rush, try pulling down the peak or brim so that the ball you are trying to rush is no longer within your peripheral vision.

Practice Exercises

Try first with a 'dolly' rush, i.e. the balls are only a few inches apart on a smooth patch of lawn and try not to hit too hard. Be content to rush the target ball a few yards until you can do this consistently, then increase the strength of the shot until you can dolly rush a ball the length of the court. Remember that to hit harder, it is better to swing longer with the same rhythm than to try to force the shot and lose the consistency of the swing.

When you have mastered the dolly rush, increase the distance between the balls gradually. Do not be too ambitious; remember your objective is consistent success. Then extend your practice so that you have a definite target to rush to. Start with the balls at hoop 4 and practise straight rushes to hoop 5. When you have got the range, try a slightly-angled cut rush and increase the angle gradually to about 45 degrees. Repeat the whole exercise, this time rushing from hoop 4 to hoop 1.

If you have difficulty getting the direction of a cut rush right, it could be that you are not seeing the right line. Place a second ball in contact with the target ball so that the line joining the centres is in the direction of the required rush. Then place a third ball about a foot beyond the second ball and in line with it and the striker's ball. Now remove the second ball and aim at the third ball. Provided that your swing is accurate, you will get the rush in the right direction.

THE TAKE-OFF

General Principles *(Fig 31)*

When you have roqueted a ball successfully, your own ball becomes a ball in hand and is picked up after it comes to rest. It is then placed in contact with the ball that has just been roqueted (replacing the latter on the yard-line, if it has been knocked into the yard-line area or off the court) and croquet is taken by striking your own ball once again.

Care must be taken with any croquet shot to ensure that neither ball is sent off the court, for this would end the striker's turn unless his ball happened to make another roquet or run its correct hoop during the stroke before leaving the court. (Note: the technical difference between stroke and striking period is that although both begin when the striker swings with intent to hit the ball, the stroke ends when all the balls have come to rest, whereas the striking period ends when the striker has quit his stance under control.) The turn also ends if, during the striking period, the striker touches any ball other than his own with his mallet or plays away from and fails to move or shake the croqueted ball.

With a croquet stroke the swing angle is defined as the angle between the line of aim and the line joining the centres of the balls.

The Thin Take-off
(Figs 32–33)

This is the easiest of the croquet strokes to play because it is the one most like a single-ball stroke. The objective is to send your ball to some desired position on the court without moving the other ball very far. Your ball is placed in contact with the other ball in such a way that the line joining their centres is at right angles to the direction in which the take-off is required to travel.

You are allowed to touch the roqueted ball to make it hold its position, provided that its position and orientation are not disturbed. It is sometimes difficult to get the two balls to stay in contact on an imperfect surface; in this case remove your ball and use your thumb to create a small depression to the side of the other ball so that your ball will nestle against it when replaced. This is much more effective than pressing down heavily on both balls in an effort to get them to stay together and is kinder to the lawn surface.

It is also permissible to use your mallet as a guide in setting up the balls for the croquet stroke by placing it in contact with the two balls with the shaft pointing in the required direction. However, once you have got beyond the beginner stage, this practice should be avoided (it looks awkward and slows down the game) unless there is a need for particular accuracy. Most players quickly learn to judge the required position of the balls by eye.

In order to move the other ball, the line of aim should be a few degrees in towards it, i.e. the swing angle is almost 90 degrees. The swing should be as for a single-ball

Fig 31 The take-off: William Prichard's elegant side style.

stroke and the reaction between the two balls will send the take-off almost exactly in the required direction. Unless you have a particular reason for moving the croqueted ball as little as possible (for example, you may want to leave it in a wired position) you should always aim to move it a few inches. As a rough guide, an inch or two per yard of take-off will be adequate. This will avoid the possibility of an imperfect swing failing to move the croqueted ball at all and will also clear it out of the way before it can be struck by the mallet, should the latter twist on impact.

The only other thing is to judge the strength of the stroke. Because the croqueted ball moves so little, it is almost the same strength as that required to send a single ball the same distance. It is worth becoming a good judge of pace with the thin take-off. More often than not you will use the thin take-off to get your ball close to another ball in preparation for a roquet or a rush. It makes a lot of difference to your confidence in shooting, if you can get within 3yd (2.7m) rather than 10yd (9m). As a rule of thumb, you should be able to send a take-off consistently to within about ten per cent of the desired distance. Players with a good touch can do much better than this.

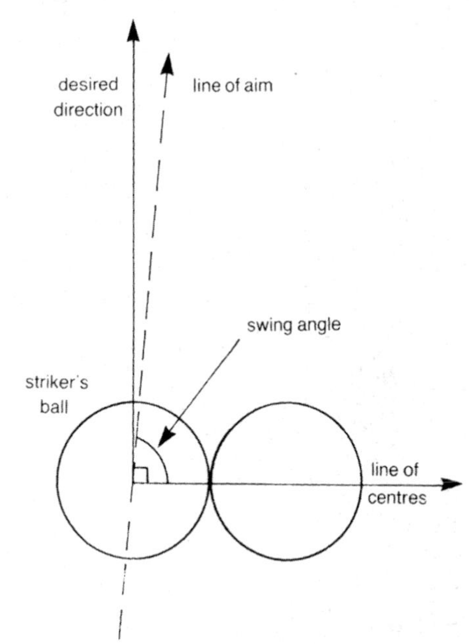

Fig 32 Thin take-off.

Fig 33 The thin take-off.

Practice Exercises

Put a target ball 5yd (4.5m) in from the yard-line and play half a dozen thin take-offs, aiming to get just beyond but not more than 1yd (91cm) beyond the target ball. Now turn around and play half a dozen take-offs back within the yard-line, remembering that in play your turn ends if the ball goes off the court. (Note: a ball is off the court as soon as any part of it touches the vertical plane defined by the inner edge of the boundary line.) If you send a ball off the court whilst

Fig 34 Using the mallet to line up an extremely fine take-off. Note the corner flag may be removed if it impedes the swing.

practising, as a penalty start the whole exercise again. Although the distance of the shot is the same, the presence of the boundary can be quite inhibiting and you will probably find that your take-offs will tend to fall short. Practise getting behind a yard-line ball from different distances, to establish the maximum distance at which you can guarantee to get behind the ball without going off the court. You will need to know this distance for match play.

For longer take-offs choose suitable targets, for example hoop 1 to the peg, hoop 1 to hoop 2 or across the court from one boundary to the other. Check to see whether you are consistently within the ten per cent margin of error. Practise take-offs from both sides of the ball. It is surprising how many players prefer taking off from one particular side.

The Extremely Thin Take-off *(Fig 34)*

There are rare occasions when you will have to play a much thinner take-off than normal. One example is when you have roqueted your ball into a corner and are faced with a take-off to your opponent's balls on the boundary near the diagonally opposite corner. This is a distance of some 40yd (36.5m) and there is clearly a danger of sending the croqueted ball off the court, particularly if the boundary is not safe (the court slopes down to the boundary) and there is a lot of furniture (court equipment) in the way.

This is a case when even the expert players use their mallets to line up the balls carefully, so do not be afraid to do so yourself. When you are satisfied that the balls are lined up accurately, leave your mallet on the ground and stand back a couple of yards to select some point of aim for your swing which is slightly to the inward side of the direction for the take-off. Pick up your mallet and check that the balls are still in contact, then stalk the ball as if you intended to shoot at your previously selected point of aim. With practice, you will barely shake the croqueted ball even on a long take-off.

If you intend to play a take-off as fine as this in a match, you should ask for someone to referee the shot. The extremely thin take-off should be reserved for the special occasions when it is essential and should not be used for normal play. There is far too much danger of committing a fault by not moving or shaking the croqueted ball. Even if you do consistently shake the ball, it will not be obvious to your opponent or to spectators and you may get a bad reputation.

Fig 35 The thick take-off.

The Thick Take-off

(Fig 35 and 36)

It is a characteristic of all take-offs that the striker's ball travels further than the croqueted ball and this is still true for the thick take-off, where the angle of swing can be anything between 45 and 80 degrees. The intention with this stroke is not only to send your ball to the desired position, but also to move the croqueted ball some distance to a more favourable position.

You have probably noticed that your ball does not go exactly at right angles to the line joining to the two balls, when you play a long, thin take-off. Apart from the reaction of the two balls, there is also the effect of the mallet swinging at an angle, causing the path of your ball to be dragged in the direction of the swing. (Note: strangely, there is no commonly accepted name for this effect, although it is often called pull.

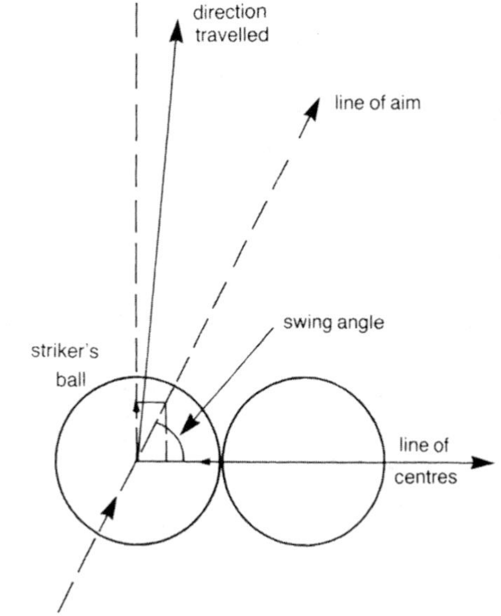

Fig 36 Thick take-off.

Perhaps this is a bit of a misnomer, for the ball is more pushed than pulled but, in any case, push and pull are technical terms for faults in a croquet stroke where the striker's ball is guided by the mallet after the croqueted ball has departed. Pull is also the name given to a different effect on the croqueted ball.) The effect is very slight in the case of the thin take-off and is easily allowed for when aligning the balls.

With a thick take-off, however, the effect of drag is much more pronounced, as the mallet is now swinging much more in the direction of the other ball. The magnitude of this effect depends mainly upon the swing angle, but also upon the weight of the mallet, the strength of the grip and follow-through just after impact. With a very thick take-off it can amount to several yards over the length of the court and can only be determined for each individual by practice.

Also, because you are now trying to move two balls instead of one, you will have to hit much harder to get your ball to travel the same distance as a thin take-off. How much harder you must hit depends upon the thickness of the take-off and, again, can only be determined by practice and experience.

The thick take-off is, therefore, a more difficult shot to play than a thin take-off and, because of this, tends to be neglected by high-bisquers and middle-bisquers. Nevertheless, it is an extremely valuable shot to have at your command and not so difficult that it is not worth acquiring.

With all croquet strokes you should keep the mallet swinging in the same plane throughout the stroke including the follow-through. In the thick take-off there is a natural tendency to follow the path of the ball with the mallet. This is not necessarily a fault, unless you are guiding the ball after the croqueted ball has gone, but it looks ugly and is less consistent. If you start to swing the mallet round before impact, then you will have to rely upon perfect timing to get consistent results.

Practice Exercises

The first thing to establish is how much your ball is dragged in a thick take-off with your particular style. Put two balls in contact on the south boundary about 4yd (3.6m) in from the first corner. Aim towards hoop 6 – this will give a swing angle of just under 70 degrees – and play the thick take-off sufficiently hard to send your ball over the north boundary, noting where it crosses the boundary. (Note: it helps to do this practice with a partner, playing thick take-offs alternately from opposite boundaries. Not only will you be able to note the amount of drag more accurately with the help of your partner, but you will also save a lot of walking about after the balls.) Do not worry at this stage about keeping the ball in court – that will come later.

When you are getting a consistent result, line the balls up so that a thin take-off would send the ball as much to the left as the drag on the thick take-off has been taking it to the right. Aim now a little to the left of hoop 6, to allow for the new orientation of the balls and play the thick take-off again. You should now find that the ball travels more or less straight up the court parallel to the west boundary. Now you can adjust the strength of the stroke so that the ball remains in play, coming to rest perhaps between hoop 2 and the north boundary. Observe how far the croqueted ball has travelled. You should then be able to judge by simple proportions the distance each ball will travel with a 70-degree thick take-off, whatever the strength of the stroke.

Repeat the exercise, this time aiming towards the peg, to give a 60-degree thick take-off. These two angles will give you a fair idea of what to expect when you need to play a thick take-off in a game, but you can, of course, practise with other angles. Make thick take-offs a regular feature of your practice routine and you will not regret it.

STRAIGHT CROQUET STROKES

General Principles
(Figs 37–9)

The swing angle for the straight croquet stroke is zero or very close to zero, in contrast to the thin take-off with its swing angle close to 90 degrees. The balls are lined up, therefore, so that the line of centres and the line of aim coincide and the two balls will travel in the same direction after impact. In general, the croqueted ball will travel farther than the striker's ball, the actual distance depending upon the type and strength of the stroke. The distance the striker's ball travels relative to that of the croqueted ball depends upon a number of factors, and control of this ratio of distances is crucial to success in playing breaks in croquet.

The most important factor in determining the ratio of distances for a given type of ball is the effective weight of the mallet; a heavy mallet will give a smaller ratio than a light one. The other factors are the strength of the grip and follow-through just after impact, the flexibility of the shaft and the position of the hands on the shaft. If the grip is firm and the follow-through strong just after impact, the effective weight of the mallet is increased because some of the player's body-weight is transmitted via the grip and the shaft to the mallet head. A rigid shaft will aid this transfer of body-weight more than a flexible

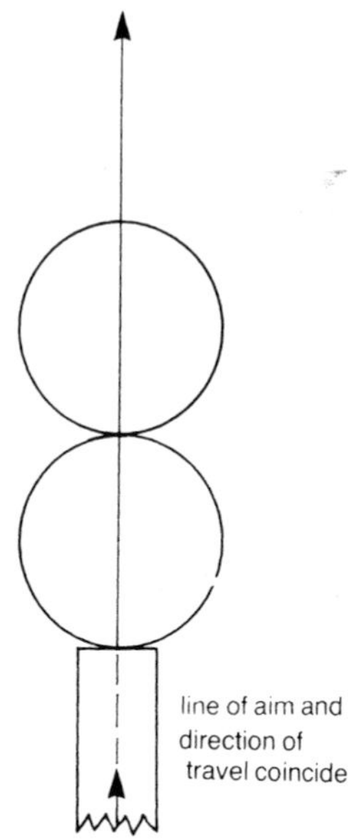

Fig 37 Straight croquet stroke.

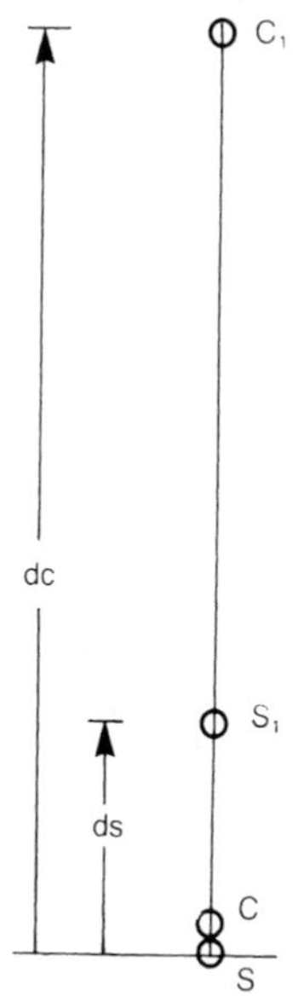

Fig 38 Distance ratio.

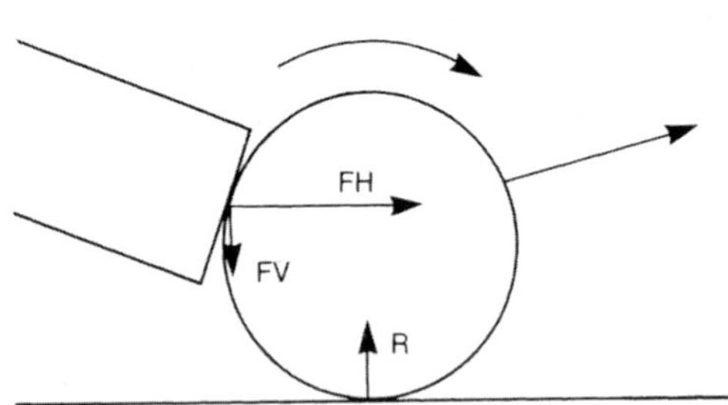

Fig 39 Inducing forward spin.

Fig 40 The drive just after impact.

one and holding the mallet lower down the shaft will reduce its flexibility.

To some extent, forward spin can be induced on to the striker's ball by hitting downwards on the ball, squeezing it between the mallet and the turf. As the friction between turf and ball is usually greater than that between mallet and ball, the ball will skip forward, spinning in the forward direction.

The basic straight croquet stroke is the straight drive; when the ratio of distances is greater than that for the straight drive, the stroke is known as a stop shot and, when the ratio is less, the stroke becomes a roll.

The Straight Drive *(Fig 40)*

The mallet is held with normal grip and hand position and the swing is exactly as if you were hitting a single ball. (Note: players who use the Solomon grip often change to a standard grip for all croquet strokes because it is difficult to play rolls with the Solomon grip; however, the drive and stop shot can be played successfully without changing grip.) The grip and follow-through should be firm, although the actual distance the mallet travels in the follow-through will be reduced because of the increased reaction from causing two balls to move.

Practice Exercises

It is vital to know the ratio of distances you normally achieve with a straight drive and that this ratio should be reasonably constant, regardless of the strength of the shot. Your choice of shot when playing will be based upon the ratio for the drive and, if the ratio varies with the strength of the shot, your decisions will become more complicated.

Take a couple of sets of balls and play gentle straight drives, aiming to get the croqueted ball to travel to a marker 10yd (9m) away. When you can achieve this consistently, check how far your ball has travelled by pacing out the distance.

Repeat this exercise for distances of approximately 20 and 30yd (18 and 27m). Hoop 1 to hoop 2 is 21yd (19m) and a spot on the east boundary opposite hoop 4 to hoop 2 is about 29yd (26m). The latter is a most useful distance for high-bisquers to practise for handicap openings; but check that the ratio is consistent. You may find that at the shorter distances the ratio is lower because you are holding back on the shot a little in an endeavour to hit gently. It is much better with gentle shots to hit with a normal, but shorter, swing rather than to try to reduce the mallet head speed from a longer swing. Remember to follow through normally and keep the grip firm throughout the shot.

On no account try to follow through more than normal, particularly if the grip is weak. There would then be a danger that you would push the ball, that is keep contact with the ball long after the croqueted ball has departed, or that you would double-tap, that is, hit the ball twice; both of these are faults and would mean the end of your turn in a game.

The drive ratio will usually be between 3:1 and 4:1, i.e. your ball will travel between one-third and one-quarter of the distance of the croqueted ball. The drive ratio is determined primarily by the head weight and balance of the mallet.

If you find that you are achieving a ratio much less than 3:1, it is probable that your mallet is very heavy. Whilst this does not matter too much for the drive, you will find it impossible to play a good stop shot with a very heavy mallet. Weigh your mallet on some kitchen scales, or let a more experienced player try it to give you his opinion.

The Stop Shot *(Figs 41–3)*

Once the knack of playing the stop shot has been acquired, it is one of the most satisfying shots to play and one of the most accurate; because the striker's ball does not travel very far, its position can be controlled more easily. Expert players often rush a ball into a position where a stop shot can be played as the next croquet stroke.

There are two ways to play the stop shot, depending upon your level of skill. The easy way is to swing normally until just before impact, then relax the grip completely and stop swinging. In this way no body-weight is transferred into the shot, only the weight of the mallet has any effect. This way also has the advantage that you can play the stop shot with your hands in the normal position.

The better way to play the shot and the way which will give a better ratio of distances, is to ground the heel of the mallet on impact to prevent any follow-through of the mallet. The mallet should also be gripped as close as possible to the top of the shaft, to allow its full flexibility to come into play.

Take up your normal stance behind the ball, then step back about 2in (5cm), pulling back on the top of the shaft of the mallet but leaving the mallet head in position on the ground. This will tilt the shaft backwards and raise the front of the mallet head by about half an inch. Swing as normal until just before impact and then, with a loose but not completely relaxed grip, push the mallet down vertically to the ground so that the heel of the mallet makes contact simultaneously with the impact.

This is a complicated manoeuvre and one

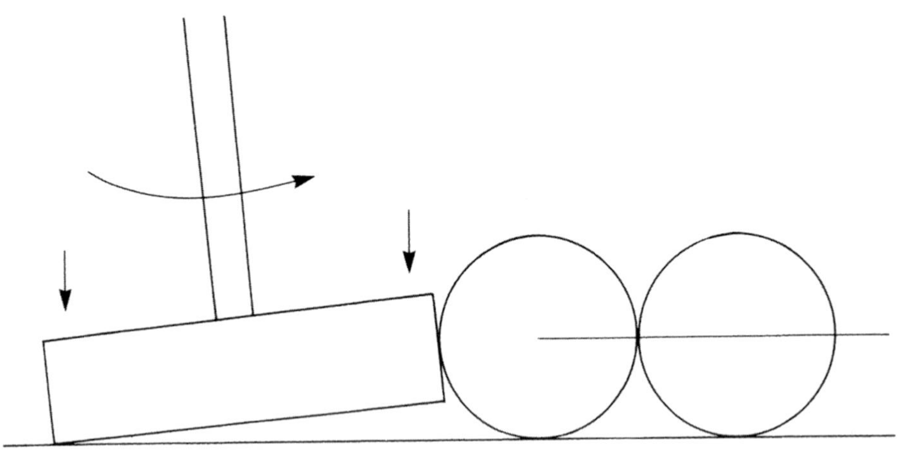

Fig 41 Stop shot: grounding the mallet.

Fig 42 The stop shot: note the grounded heel of the mallet; the back ball has just left the ground.

that requires accurate timing. If you ground the mallet head too early, you will, at best, take some of the strength out of the shot and, at worst, may even fail to hit the ball. If you are too late in grounding the mallet, you will not achieve a good stop-shot ratio.

Nevertheless, it is worth practising this method. It will give you a much better stop-shot ratio than the simpler method, because it prevents any follow-through of the mallet head. In addition, the ball is struck with a slightly tilted mallet and the reaction between the balls and the mallet will cause the striker's ball to leave the ground with a small amount of backspin.

It is important to keep the stop-shot swing as smooth as possible, in spite of its more complicated nature. This will assist the timing of the shot. Too many players play the shot with a kind of wristy jab with unpredictable results.

As a refinement to this technique when a particularly good stop shot is required, some players aim to hit the ball slightly off-centre. The mallet twists on impact reducing the force on the back ball after the front ball has gone. However, the back ball will squirt out slightly sideways in a manner which is difficult to control, and this technique should not normally be employed. (*See* Fig 43.)

As a general guide, stop shots with a ratio of 5:1 can be readily achieved with the simple method and 6:1 with the grounding method. Experts, particularly if they play with a fibreglass shaft, can attain ratios as good as 10:1.

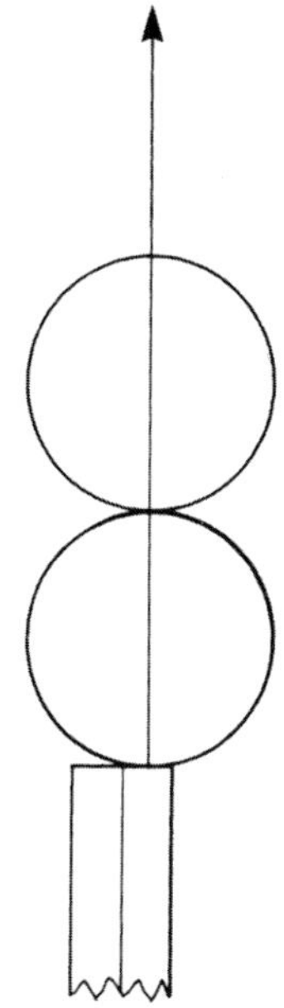

Fig 43 Hitting off-centre.

Practice Exercises

Start your practice with gentle stop shots, as these are the easiest. Try to send the front ball about 5yd (4.5m) to a marker and see how far the back ball goes. It should be less than 1yd (91cm). Concentrate on playing a smooth stroke, whichever method you adopt, until you can attain consistent results. Extend the distance to 10, 20 and 30yd (9, 18 and 27m). One particularly useful target distance is the shot which puts a pioneer to hoop 2 from the south boundary, leaving the back ball in position to roquet a pioneer a yard in front of hoop 1.

General Principles of the Roll *(Fig 44)*

Fig 44 Phil Cordingley gets down to the roll.

There is always a temptation to follow through strongly with the roll, as the roll is the direct opposite of the stop shot with its absence of follow-through. However, this temptation should be resisted, because it could lead to an illegal push shot. The push is defined as maintaining contact between mallet and ball for an appreciable period or accelerating the mallet head if it has been checked after its initial contact with the ball. In other words, you must not continue to accelerate your ball once the croqueted ball has departed. In order to avoid the push, all roll shots should be played without excessive follow-through.

Rolls may be defined by the distance ratio of the two balls. The most usual ones are the half roll, the three-quarter roll, the full roll and the pass roll. However, any ratio can be played. As you might expect, the correct way to reduce the distance ratio below that of the drive is to reduce the flexibility of the shaft by gripping lower down or to induce some forward spin on the back ball by hitting down on to it. Most good players use a combination of the two techniques.

Over comparatively short distances rolls other than full and pass rolls can be played without forward spin, but it is difficult with a very short grip to generate sufficient mallet head speed for the longer rolls without pushing the back ball.

With full and pass rolls, particularly when they are played strongly, the impulse from the mallet transmitted through the striker's ball sends the croqueted ball ahead by a few yards. However, the croqueted ball is not rolling initially and it loses two-sevenths of its velocity by the time it is rolling fully. In contrast, the striker's ball is already rolling forward on leaving the mallet and does not decelerate as rapidly. The striker's ball quickly catches up with or passes the croqueted ball.

Although half and three-quarter rolls can be played from a standing position, the shortened grip makes it more comfortable to assume a crouched position. This, in turn, usually means that one foot has to be in front of the other to maintain balance during the stroke. The weight is mainly on the front foot. A right-handed player has the left foot forwards and vice-versa.

The standard grip is used for all roll strokes, i.e. the lower hand has the palm at the back of the mallet shaft facing forwards and the upper hand holds the shaft with knuckles to the front. The grip with the lower hand should be particularly firm to prevent any twisting of the mallet. As the roll ratio increases, the action becomes more of a drive forwards and downwards with both hands and arms rather than a swing. The mallet shaft is inclined forwards and sideways across the body.

The Half Roll *(Fig 45)*

Hold the mallet with the lower hand half-way down the shaft and the upper hand in a comfortable position below the top of the shaft. The stroke is played with the ball about 4in (10cm) forward of the toe of the front foot. The stance is slightly crouched and the mallet shaft has only a small inclination forwards. The exact position of the lower hand and the inclination of the mallet are interdependent; the lower the position of the hand, the less the mallet needs to be inclined.

The half roll can be played from the standing position. The mallet is gripped rather higher up the shaft than for the crouched position, but it is much more inclined forwards. The ball is only just in front of the front foot. The ball is struck a sharp downwards blow exerting pressure with the lower hand to squeeze the ball between turf and mallet. With this kind of shot the ball skips noticeably in the air.

Practice Exercises

Place suitable markers at distances of 5 and 10yd (4.5 and 9m). Practise half rolls, adjust-

Fig 45 The half roll: standing position.

Fig 46(a) The three-quarter roll: side view.

ing your hand position or the inclination of the mallet until you can play half rolls accurately and comfortably. You should feel that the stroke is not restrained or impeded in any way. Only when you are satisfied with this half roll, extend the distances by hitting harder but keeping the same action. Useful markers for the greater distances are: hoop 5 to hoop 6 and peg (14 and 7yd (12.8 and 6.4m)); hoop 1 to hoop 2 and opposite the peg (21 and 10.5yd (19 and 9.5m)); hoop 1 to hoop 3 and peg (25 and 12.5yd (22 and 11.2m)).

The Three-Quarter Roll *(Fig 46)*

The half roll is the starting point for your experiments with other rolls. Once you have found the hand position and inclination of the mallet for half rolls then you can quickly

(b) front view; note the mallet slanted across the body.

Fig 47(a) The full roll.

(b) The back ball has skipped up due to the chop action.

adapt to other rolls by modifying this basic position. For the three-quarter roll move both hands down the shaft a little more and incline the mallet further forwards. The ball can be played a little more towards the front foot.

The three-quarter roll can also be played from a standing position by inclining the mallet even more, but this is about the limit at which a roll can be played easily and accurately from the standing position.

Practice Exercises

Place suitable markers at distances of 8 and 6yd (7.2 and 5.5m). Play the three-quarter roll until you have mastered the technique and then gradually extend the distances to 24 and 18yd (21.5 and 16m).

The Full Roll *(Fig 47)*

Carry on the progression from the three-quarter roll by moving the hands further down the shaft and inclining the mallet more. Take care, however, that your lower hand is not touching the mallet head, as this is a fault. In fact, it is not only unnecessary but also a disadvantage to have the hands too low. It makes it far too difficult to play a big full roll cleanly. Remember that the follow-through should not be excessive. The ball should be played from just in front of the leading foot.

Practice Exercises

Firstly, practise the full roll over a short distance, but do not worry too much if the balls do not travel the same distance. At this stage it is more important to determine whether you can cleanly play a long full roll, say 20 to 25yd (18 to 22m), with the same technique. If you find the long roll impossible to achieve without a big follow-through, move your hands back up the shaft a little and chop down on the ball more. Then practise over different distances.

The Pass Roll *(Fig 48)*

As its name implies, the pass roll is used to send the striker's ball further than the croqueted ball. Remember, however, that it is not legal to accelerate the striker's ball after the croqueted ball has departed. It follows, therefore, that the only valid way to play a pass roll cleanly is to impart forward spin.

There is a limit to the amount of forward spin that can be imparted to the back ball and, therefore, a limit to the degree of pass that can be achieved. The maximum pass-roll ratio which can be achieved in theory for a straight pass roll is approximately 2:1. However, this theoretical maximum neglects the effect of the elasticity of the balls, and I would suggest that, in practice, the limit is about 1.2:1, i.e. the back ball travels 20 per cent further than the front ball. Better ratios can be achieved with a long follow-through or by employing a flicking technique where the mallet face is turned sharply upwards with the wrists on impact, but both methods are questionable. It is better not to be too ambitious with pass rolls and to be content with a modest degree of pass.

The hands should be in roughly the same position as for the full roll but the mallet should be more steeply inclined and the stroke played with a pronounced chop into the back of the ball. To prevent the mallet head following through into the turf, it helps if the point of contact on the mallet is below the centre of the face.

Practice Exercises

The pass roll is actually rather difficult to play gently because of the need to chop down into the ball quite strongly to get any forward spin. Fortunately, short pass rolls are rarely required, so it is better to practise the intermediate distances. Although it is a spectacular shot and one which you need on occasions to be able to play, do not spend too high a proportion of your practice time on the pass roll. Your time would be better spent on perfecting the more basic shots.

Fig 48 The pass roll.

SPLIT CROQUET STROKES

General Principles
(Figs 49 and 50)

The split croquet stroke is played with a swing angle between 0 and 45 degrees. At the lower end of the swing-angle range it merges into the straight croquet stroke and at the upper end into the thick take-off. There is considerable variety in the way the stroke can be played and this makes it one of the most interesting in the game.

The player who has a proper command of the split will find it extremely useful in building a break and maintaining it without the need for long roquets. Paradoxically though, because of its complication, it is a stroke which should only be played when absolutely necessary, and break play should be planned to incorporate easier strokes as far as possible.

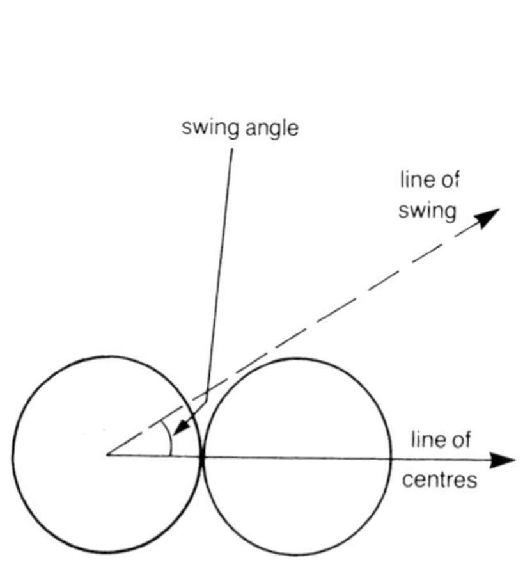

Fig 49 Split croquet stroke.

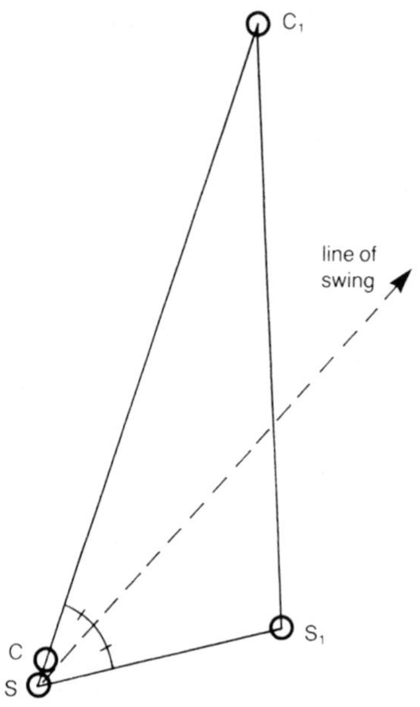

Fig 50 Splitting the angle.

With the croquet strokes discussed so far there has only been one variable in the play of the stroke; either the swing angle, as in the case of the take-off; or the manner of striking the ball, as in the case of the straight croquet stroke. With the split the complications arise from the fact that both of these variables come into play.

The starting point for the split is to visualise the final positions of the two balls that are required after the stroke has been played and the position from which the stroke will be played as the vertices of a triangle. The line of centres will point along one side of this triangle, the intended direction of the striker's ball will form another and the third side will be the line connecting the two balls when they have come to rest. For a first approximation, the line of swing can be determined by splitting the angle between the first two sides of the triangle. Some players make the aiming point for the swing the mid-point of the third side of the triangle, but this only works well for large swing angles.

The next problem is to determine the strength and type of stroke required to send the balls over the correct, relative distances. As one might expect, if the stroke is played with a stop-shot action, the relative distance of the croqueted ball with respect to the striker's ball will be greater than is the case if the stroke is played with a roll action. In addition, the swing angle has an effect on these relative distances; at greater swing angles the striker's ball will travel further with respect to the croqueted ball.

Many players have a tendency to follow through or even play the stroke in an arc with the mallet guiding the back ball along the required direction. This not only looks inelegant but can also be considered as a fault known as a push. Particular care should be taken with all split croquet stokes played with a roll action. It is very easy to trap the back ball with the inclined mallet so that it travels directly along the line of swing without any reaction from the croqueted ball. This also constitutes a push.

Pull *(Fig 51)*

As if these difficulties were not enough, the reaction between the mallet, balls and turf produces a further effect on the croqueted ball, generally known as pull.

We have already seen in the case of the thick take-off that the reaction between the mallet and the ball drags the striker's ball in towards the line of swing. In the case of the split croquet stroke, the distortion produced in the striker's ball by the impact of the mallet and the friction between the milled surfaces of the two balls pulls the path of the croqueted ball away from the line of centres towards the line of swing.

Pull is a complicated phenomenon. Its magnitude depends upon the swing angle and the type of stroke played. In general, the magnitude of the pull effect becomes greater as the type of stroke progresses from stop shot to pass roll and as the swing angle increases from 0 to about 25 degrees. The effect decreases if the swing angle is increased from approximately 25 to 45 degrees. To some extent, slow, damp courts produce more pull than fast, dry ones.

The best you can do is to make some allowance for pull, even if you cannot determine accurately in advance how great the effect will be. It is all a matter of experience and, fortunately, the normal margins of error in playing shots make it unnecessary to carry out complicated calculations. Just remember that your initial triangle needs to have a rather larger angle because of pull.

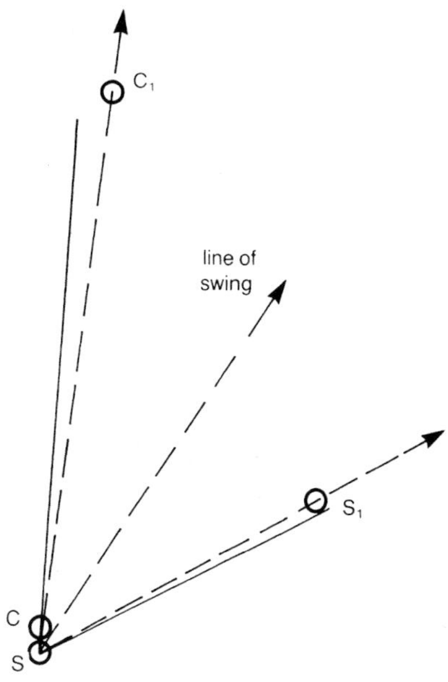

Fig 51 Effect of pull and drag

Practice Exercises (Fig 52)

The range of split croquet strokes is so great that it is impossible to cover them all. The following exercise will build up your feel for the type of stroke to be played.

Start first of all with a straight drive sending the croqueted ball about 10yd (9m). Mark the positions of the two balls and the mid-point between the initial and final positions of the croqueted ball with suitable coins. Then play splits from various positions on the quadrant of the circle passing through the starting point for the straight drive with the mid-point coin as centre. Play the shot with your normal drive. As you go round the circle, the swing angle increases, as does the relative distance travelled by the striker's ball. Try to get each ball as close as possible to the marker coins and make a

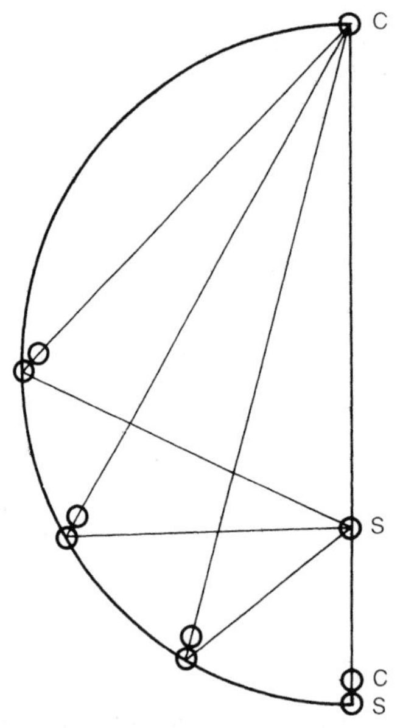

Fig 52 Split-stroke practice.

mental note of the outcome of each shot. Then adjust your technique by playing with a roll or stop shot to improve each shot. When you are confident about these shots, increase the practice distance.

There are certain splits which are worth extra practice; these are the strokes which will enable you to continue a three-ball break when you have failed to get a useful rush after running a hoop. Start at hoop 4 and practise the split to hoops 5 and 6.

A more difficult split is that from hoop 2 to hoops 3 and 4. Practise this split first on the assumption that you have a good pioneer at hoop 3, then extend the practice to the cases where you have a pioneer 2 or 3yd (1.8 or 2.7m) to the east and the west of the hoop and want to get a rush to hoop 3.

The most difficult are the splits from hoop 1 to hoops 2 and 3, played with a strong three-quarter roll, and from hoop 3 to hoops 4 and 5, played with a pass roll.

All of these splits are played so that the croqueted ball will go to the right of your line of aim and it will be pulled towards the left. Their equivalents, sending the croqueted ball to the left of the line of aim with pull to the right, are: 4-back to penult and rover; 2-back to 3-back and 4-back; 1-back to 2-back and 3-back; and 3-back to 4-back and penult. These should also be practised.

4 Applied Technique

HOOP APPROACHES

(Figs 53–8)

The ability to make a good hoop approach from a difficult position will make it possible for you to continue a break with the greatest of ease and will often rescue a break which has got into difficulties. In the first case, we define a good hoop approach as one which will enable you to run the hoop with control, and these can only be made with confidence if you are reasonably close to the hoop; in the second case, you may find yourself a long way away from the hoop, and a good approach is one which gives you a sporting chance of running the hoop.

In play, the hoop approach should be carefully planned to put the croqueted ball in a useful position. Too many players have

Fig 53 The hoop approach.

Fig 54(a) A hoop approach by Robert Fulford.

Fig 54(b) It leaves an easy hoop.

discovered that they can make reasonable hoop approaches with one particular shot – for beginners it is often the roll – and therefore use this approach every time, regardless of whether or not it is the correct stroke to play. A characteristic of this type of player is the way he looks round after running the hoop to see what to do next. A good player will know what he intends to do after running the hoop *before* he has played the hoop approach and will play the stroke which will make it easiest to carry out his plan.

As an example, if you are approaching hoop 1, it is most probable that you would like a forward rush after running the hoop. A full roll is definitely not the shot to play here, even if it is your favourite hoop approach. On the other hand, the approach to hoop 2

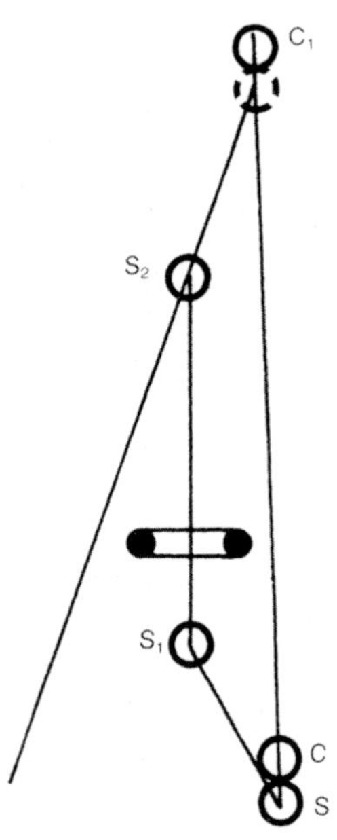

Fig 55 Stop-shot approach for forward rush.

may well require a roll, because you would probably like a rush back into the court.

It follows, therefore, that you need to be versatile with your hoop approaches, not only in the play of the stroke but also with your planning of where to put the croqueted ball.

Let us consider three particular cases where you want (a) a forward rush, (b) a sideways rush and (c) a rush back into court. We shall make it easy as well and suppose that you are within a foot of the hoop. In case (a) you plan to put your ball within 6in (15cm) of the hoop, which means you must play a stop shot to get the croqueted ball sufficiently far down the court to get the rush. However, if you play a stop shot which puts the croqueted ball, say, 1yd (1m) past the hoop and dead in front, you may find yourself with a beautiful, straight dolly rush after running the hoop, but with a severely impeded back swing. The approach, therefore, should still be a stop shot but not placing the croqueted ball dead in front of the hoop. Play for an easy cut rush by playing the croqueted ball slightly to one side.

In case (b) you clearly want to put the croqueted ball to one side of the hoop but how far to the side? If you place it just to the side and a couple of feet past, you will have to be extremely accurate in your hoop running to get a reasonable sideways rush; 6in (15cm) too far or too short will leave a very nasty cut rush. Play a stop shot instead, to put the croqueted ball a couple of feet to one side, and you will still have an easy rush if everything is perfect, with a much greater margin of error, if you overhit or underhit the hoop-running stroke.

In case (c) play the croqueted ball past the hoop rather than leaving it alongside the hoop. In that way, you will still be able to play a cut rush if you run the hoop too hard, whereas the hoop may be in the way if you place the croqueted ball alongside it.

In all of these cases, you will have to change your choice of shot, the further you are away form the hoop. If you are 1yd (91cm) away, in case (a) you now have room to put the croqueted ball 2 or 3yd (1.8 or 2.7m) past the hoop with a drive, in case (b) the shot becomes more of a half roll and in case (c) a three-quarter roll. In general, the further you are away from the hoop, the more of a roll the shot becomes.

Through practice and play you should become aware of your margin of error in the position of your ball after a hoop approach.

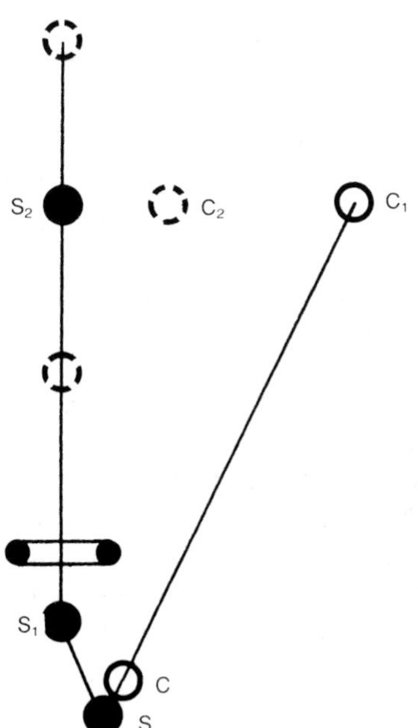

Fig 56 Hoop approach for a sideways rush.

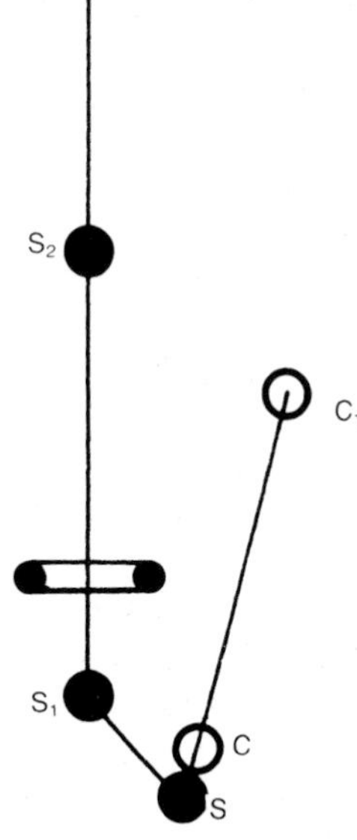

Fig 57 Hoop approach for a backwards rush.

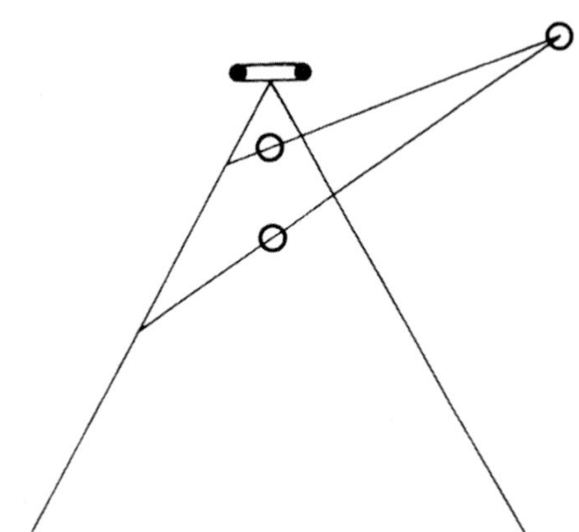

Fig 58 Margin of error

Always play your hoop approaches so that you will be able to run the hoop provided that you stay within this margin of error. This is particularly important when approaching hoops from the side. If you try to get too close to the hoop, an underhit or overhit shot will leave you with an impossibly angled hoop.

Practice Exercises (Fig 59)

Practise stop-shot hoop approaches from a semicircle, 1ft (30cm) in front of the hoop. Try to get the croqueted ball as far down the court as possible with the striker's ball coming to rest 6in (15cm) in front of the hoop. Extend the distance to 2ft (60cm). Short stop

Fig 59 Round the clock hoop-approach practice.

shots are easier to execute than long ones but it is a common error to underhit them and leave the striker's ball short of the required position.

Hoop approaches from 1 to 3yd (91cm to 2.7m) are best practised on the round the clock principle, i.e. from various positions around a circle centred on the hoop. Start first with a circle with a 1yd (91cm) radius. From each position on the semicircle in front of the hoop, play to get a forward, a sideways and a backwards rush.

The possibilities are more limited from the semicircle behind the hoop; from this side you should always practise a thick take-off to move the croqueted ball for a subsequent forward rush or a sideways rush to the other side. In games you will have ample opportunities to play thin take-offs of varying distances. To practise thin take-off hoop approaches would be a waste of valuable practice time. Beware of the temptation, when playing the thick take-off, to twist the mallet towards the hoop. Even if you are not shepherding the ball, you will probably overhit the shot. Build up your confidence in playing the shot correctly along the swing line throughout the swing. There will be times in a game when you need to play this shot.

At distances greater than 3yd (2.7m) from the wrong side of the hoop the vital thing is to get a position where you can run the hoop. In this situation the thin take-off is by far the safest shot. However, your time would be better spent practising these greater distances from the playing side of the hoop. At these distances all your concentration should be on getting in a position to run the hoop. A half to three-quarter roll will usually be best.

The maximum distance that it is worth while practising from is about 6 to 7 yd (5.5 to 6.4m). As you improve, you will not need to play as many long hoop approaches. Beginners are usually quite adept at hoop approaches from long distances because they often need to play them, whereas some experts get quite nervous if they are more than a few feet away.

CANNONS

Three-ball and Four-ball Groups *(Figs 60–3)*

An especially interesting situation occurs when the ball from which you wish to take croquet is in contact with another ball in the immediate vicinity of a yard-line. These two balls plus the striker's ball form a three-ball group if any of them are on a yard-line. In this case, both the striker's ball and the ball

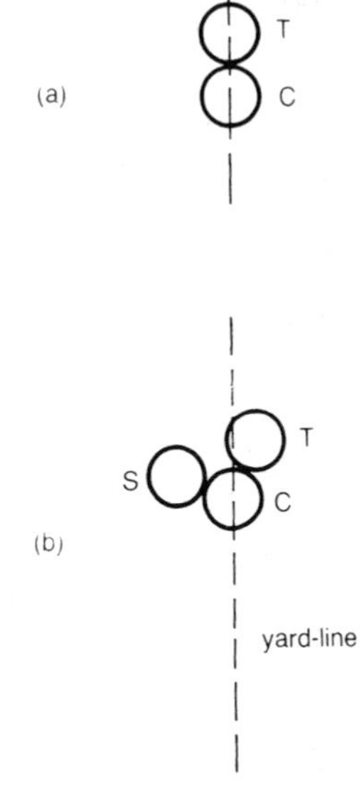

Fig 60(a) Balls in contact on yard-line.
(b) Balls arranged for cannon.

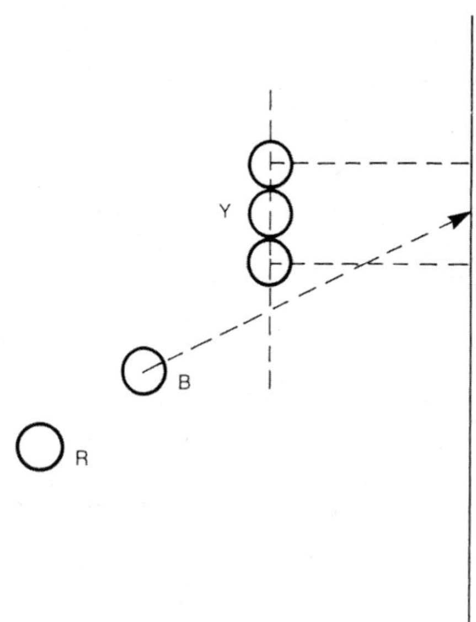

Fig 61 Getting a yard-line cannon.

Fig 62 The corner cannon.

which has not been roqueted in the preceding stroke become balls in hand, and may be placed in contact with the roqueted ball in any position, as long as they are not in contact with each other. (Note: the position of the roqueted ball may not be altered.)

If the balls are so arranged that in playing the croquet stroke a roquet is made on the third ball, the shot is called a cannon. As the third ball can be placed anywhere in contact with the roqueted ball, considerable advantage can be obtained with a cannon.

The situation usually arises when a ball is rushed into the yard-line area or off the court so that, when it is replaced, it is in contact with another yard-line ball. In general, it is easier to rush the ball off the court within the box (as shown in Fig 61) than to play the ball into the yard-line area. However, it is quite difficult to arrange this deliberately if the balls are well separated unless the third ball is a corner ball. (Note: it is much easier to rush a ball into the corner than into a more narrowly defined area on a yard-line away from the corner.) Such cannons are then called corner cannons and a number of standard cannons from corner spots make it possible to pick up a three-ball break rather easily.

A somewhat rarer situation occurs with a four-ball group, which is formed when the fourth ball is in contact with a three-ball group. In this case, the fourth ball is also a ball in hand and may be placed in contact with either or both of the roqueted and third balls, provided that it is not in contact with the striker's ball.

If a player chooses to play with a ball which is part of a three-ball or four-ball group at the beginning of his turn, he may take croquet from any of the other balls in the group. A roquet is then deemed to have been made on that ball.

In the following discussion of standard

Fig 63 The arrangement of the balls for the cannon.

cannons it will be assumed that the player is playing with red and has roqueted or is deemed to have roqueted yellow. The third ball will be assumed to be blue and is already on a corner spot. The exact outcome of the cannon for a given position of the balls will depend upon the weight of the player's mallet and the manner in which the stroke is played. The positions given in the cases below should be regarded as approximate positions to be used for experimentation.

Corner 1 – Hoop 1 Cannon

(Figs 64 and 65)

Blue was the ball originally on the corner spot and yellow has been rushed into the corner. First of all, you should place yellow on either the south or west yard-line in contact with blue. Then pick up blue and place red in contact with yellow so that their line of centres points slightly west of hoop 2.

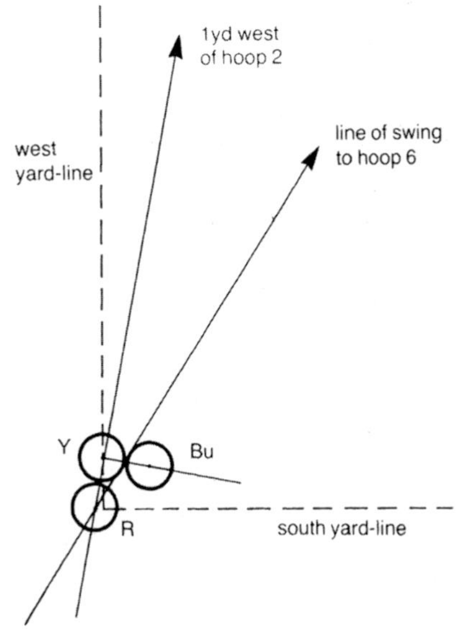

Fig 64 Corner 1 – hoop 1 cannon.

Finally you should place blue in contact with yellow so that it is at right-angles to the other two balls. (Note: if blue is dislodged from the corner spot during the course of the roquet but remains in the corner area, either blue or yellow may be placed on the corner spot. If yellow is placed on the corner spot, blue is a ball in hand and is placed in contact with yellow as above.)

Play the shot with your normal drive and with the swing line directed towards hoop 6, using sufficient strength to send yellow to hoop 2. By aiming yellow a little to the west (left) of hoop 2, you have allowed for a little pull and yellow should end up as a good pioneer at hoop 2. The red ball will also have roqueted blue, cut-rushing it towards hoop 1. If you are not satisfied with the outcome – and remember you need blue to be reasonably close to hoop 1 rather than having a perfect pioneer at hoop 2 – then you will have to experiment.

The two things you can change are the position of the blue ball and the direction of the swing. You could also change the type of stroke you employ but I do not recommend this. Your drive should be your most reliable stroke and you should use it to get consistent results.

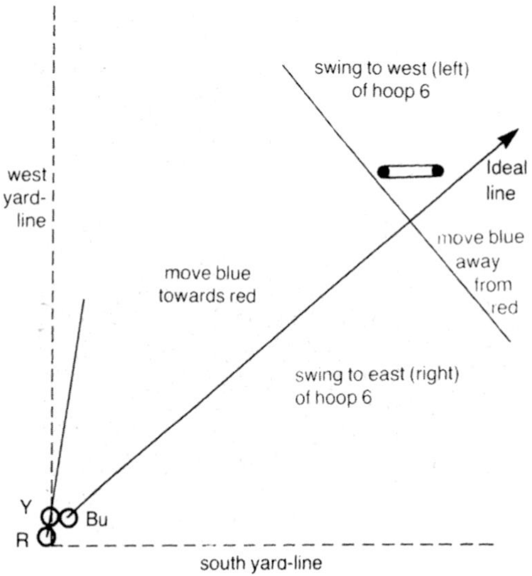

Fig 65 Improving the cannon.

Let us consider first the effect of changing the position of the blue ball. If you move the blue ball so that it is at less than a right angle, i.e. it is closer to red, then you will get less of a cut-rush on blue and it will travel further. Try this if blue is short and to the left of the line from corner 1 to a yard dead in front of hoop 1 (the ideal line). Conversely, if you place blue at more than a right angle to red and yellow, the effect will be to cut blue more and send it less distance. Try this if blue is going too far and to the right of the ideal line, but be careful that you are actually roqueting blue and not just promoting it. There will also be some reaction on yellow from blue and it will travel to the left of the intended direction.

For a given position of the balls, changing the line of swing will have the following effects. If you swing more towards the right of hoop 6, yellow will not travel as far and blue will be cut more and hit harder. Try this if blue is very short and to the right of the ideal line. Conversely, if you swing more towards the left of hoop 6, yellow will travel further and blue will be cut less but hit more gently. Try this if blue is going too far and to the left of the ideal line.

Once you have discovered the best combination for your mallet and your style, the same cannon can be played from corner 3 to hoop 3 and its mirror images – a split to the left instead of the right – from corner 2 to 1-back and from corner 4 to 3-back.

Corner 2 – Hoop 2 Cannon *(Fig 66)*

As we have seen in the discussion on the corner 1 – hoop 1 cannon the relative distances which the roqueted and croqueted balls travel can be adjusted by altering the positions of the balls and the line of swing.

This time blue is on corner 2 and yellow is roqueted into the corner 2 area. The order in which the balls are placed is exactly the same as for the previous cannon but the line of centres for red and yellow points a couple of yards north of hoop 3. Blue should be placed at right angles to red and yellow and the cannon played with the swing line directed towards the peg. The ideal line goes from red to 1yd (91cm) south of hoop 2. If the shot is not immediately successful, adjustments can be made by reference to the position of red in relation to the ideal line in the same way as for the corner 1 – hoop 1 cannon.

The mirror image of this cannon is corner 1 to 2-back.

Wafer Cannons (Figs 67 and 68)

Although it is possible in theory to play the basic right-angled cannon for shots where the rushed ball has to travel further than the croqueted ball, in practice it is very difficult to get consistent results. For this reason the wafer cannon is generally used to get the rushed ball into a reliable position, whilst

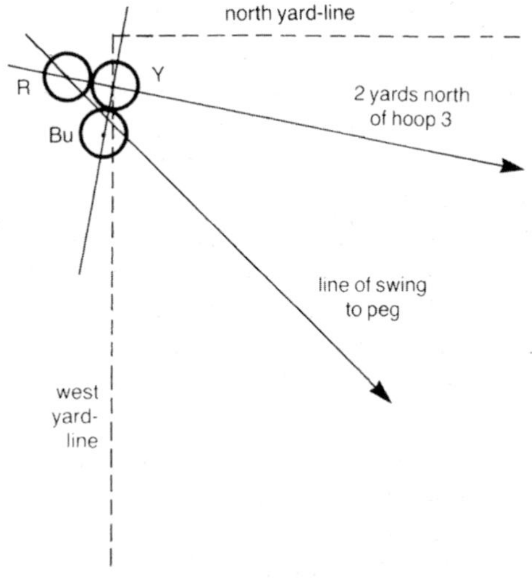

Fig 66 Corner 2 – hoop 2 cannon.

Fig 67(a) and (b) Two views of the wafer cannon: the gap between the striker's ball and the ball to be roqueted should be as small as possible.

Fig 67(b)

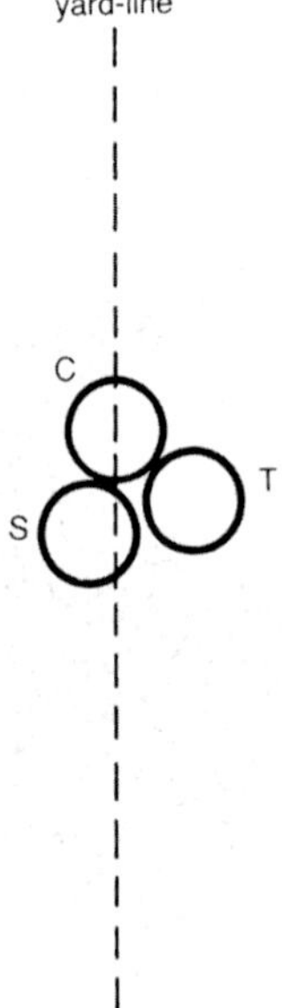

Fig 68 Wafer cannon.

sacrificing the accuracy of the croqueted ball as a pioneer.

The arrangement of the balls for a wafer cannon is such that red and blue are separated by as little as possible, i.e. there is only a wafer gap between them.

Corner 2 – Hoop 1 Cannon *(Fig 69)*
Here the line of centres of red and blue points to hoop 1. The line of centres of red and yellow will point in the direction of hoop 6. The swing line is towards hoop 1 and the stroke is played with rather more force than would be required for a dolly rush from corner 2 – hoop 1, to allow for the energy required to move yellow. Yellow will finish generally to the north-east of hoop 2.

The same cannon can be used for corner 4 – hoop 3 and its mirror image for corner 1 – 1-back and corner 3 –3-back

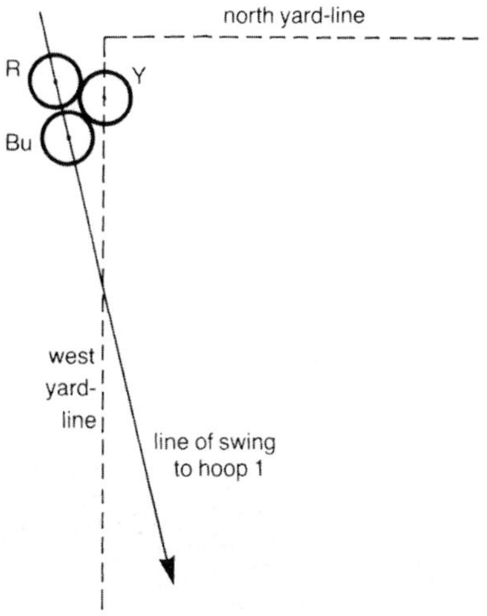

Fig 69 Corner 2 – hoop 1 wafer cannon.

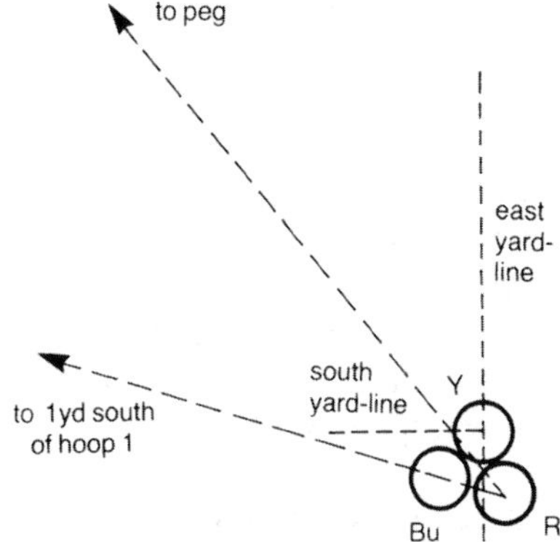

Fig 70 Corner 4 – hoop 1 cannon.

Corner 4 – Hoop 1 Cannon *(Fig 70)*
This is another cannon where the blue ball has to be rushed a long way and playing the wafer cannon is the safest shot. The line of centres for red and blue points a couple of yards south of hoop 1 and for red and yellow to the west of hoop 3.

However, note that yellow will not get anywhere near hoop 2. The swing line will depend on how far you want to bring yellow into the court. The easiest shot to judge the strength required is to swing along the line of centres of red and blue, but this will not bring yellow out much beyond hoop 4. If the swing line is directed towards the peg, yellow will be brought further into court but the force required to rush blue to a good position for hoop 1 is much greater and harder to judge accurately.

The Four-ball Cannon (Figs 71 and 72)

The four-ball cannon is difficult to contrive. It usually occurs by chance when, as a result of poor shooting on the second, third and fourth turns, all four balls are in contact on the east boundary.

Fig 71 The four-ball cannon.

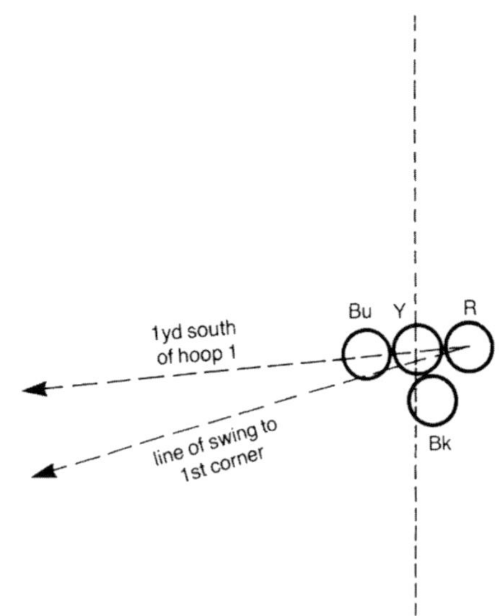

Fig 72 Four-ball cannon.

The striker's ball, the ball which is deemed to have been roqueted and a third ball are placed in a straight line so that their line of centres points to a spot 1yd (91cm) in front of hoop 1. When the shot is played, the impulse passing through the middle ball promotes the far ball to hoop 1, regardless of the direction of swing.

It is possible to place the balls for a four-ball cannon so that the promoted ball goes to hoop 2 and the rushed ball to hoop 1 or vice versa. However, these shots require considerable strength, the outcome is often unpredictable and the resistance offered by four balls is enormous. (The shots are sometimes known as mallet breakers.)

It is far safer to place the fourth ball so that it can be rushed towards the south boundary. A simple split croquet shot will then send it to hoop 2 with the striker's ball going to the promoted pioneer at hoop 1. In the cannon stroke the croqueted ball will be squeezed out towards hoop 4 and can be picked up later in the break.

PEG-OUTS AND PEELS

Pegging out *(Figs 73–5)*

At the end of the game the final act is to peg out. Provided that you are within 6 or 7yd (5.5 or 6.4m) of the peg (of course you hope to be much closer), it is almost impossible to miss if the alignment is correct; and yet people do miss peg-outs. There are two ways to line up the balls for the peg-out.

The first way is to crouch down low a few yards behind the balls and to look over the top of them. If you are looking along the correct line, you should see the nearest ball and behind it an arc of the second ball. If the balls are correctly lined up, in the background the peg will appear in line with the top of the arc of the second ball. If the peg appears to be to the left of the arc, the balls are pointing to the right of the peg and vice-versa.

The second way is to lie down and look along the tangent touching the edge of both balls. If the balls are lined up correctly, in the background you should see the peg apparently growing out of the arc of the nearer ball. Look along the tangent touching the diametrically opposite edges and you should see the same effect reversed. If the balls are not lined up correctly, you will be able to see the peg or part of it to one side of the balls.

Once you are satisfied that the alignment is correct, make absolutely certain that the balls are in contact: separation of the balls is the most probable cause of missed peg-outs. Now stalk the balls and the peg, have a last check to see that they have not separated, and hit the shot with a firm, flat drive with sufficient force to leave your ball by the peg. It may be tempting to try to roll the balls up to the peg if they are several yards away, but it is very difficult to roll two balls absolutely straight. Remember that pull has its

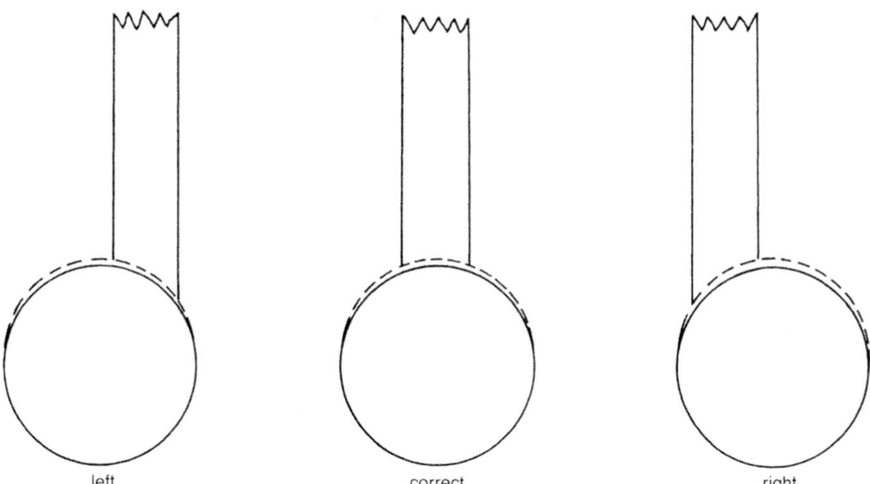

Fig 73 Peg out.

Fig 74 The peg-out: view over the tops of the balls.

Fig 75(a) The peg-out: view along the right side of the balls.

Fig 75(b) The view along the left side of the balls.

greatest effect with a roll. Take your courage in both hands, drive firmly and give yourself the best possible chance of making the peg-out.

The Peel *(Figs 76–8)*

The technique of playing your partner ball or an opposition ball through a hoop in the course of a turn is known as peeling the ball. This is generally performed with a croquet stroke, but can be done in favourable circumstances with a rush. In any event, careful preparation is required to get the ball to be peeled (the peelee) into the correct position.

The ideal position for the peelee is straight in front of the hoop and from 1ft (30cm) to 1yd (91cm) away from it, but usually the peel has to be performed from an angle. The balls are lined up, taking care to allow for pull if the peel is played with a split croquet stroke. Allowance for pull is not easy to judge,

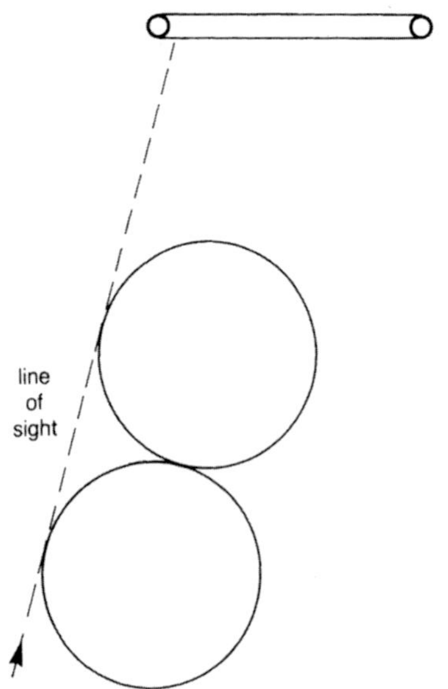

Fig 76 Lining up the angled peel.

Fig 77(a) The peel: view over the balls.
(b) The view through the hoop.

as it depends on so many factors. However, it is probable that you will have played a few split croquet strokes, for example hoop approaches, before you ever reach a peeling position. Use these opportunities to gauge how much the balls are pulling.

Of course, pull can be avoided if a straight croquet stroke can be employed. Then the alignment of the balls is arranged so that the croqueted ball will just miss the near wire when the stroke is played, in much the same way that an angled hoop is run. Different players have different techniques for the alignment procedure. Some prefer to align the balls in the same way as used for a peg-out by looking across the tops of the balls from a low position and using their experience to judge where to aim for a given angle; others like to look along the sides of the two balls to make sure that the tangent touching the two edges will miss the near wire. My own preference is for the latter method.

The peel is easiest to play with a gentle drive because the grip is quite firm. With the looser grip of a stop shot there is always a danger that the mallet will twist a little if the ball is not struck with the centre of the mallet face, causing the croqueted ball to be pulled. If the peel is played with a split or thickish take-off, it is better to over-allow for pull rather than under-allow because the side spin imparted will help the ball to spin through the hoop off the far wire. Peels that are played across the hoop are less likely to succeed because then the side spin is imparted in the wrong sense.

Remember also, your turn will come to an end if you send the peelee off the court in the croquet stroke, even if the peel is successful.

The Straight Peel

This peel refers to the situation when both the peelee and the striker's ball are for the

(b)

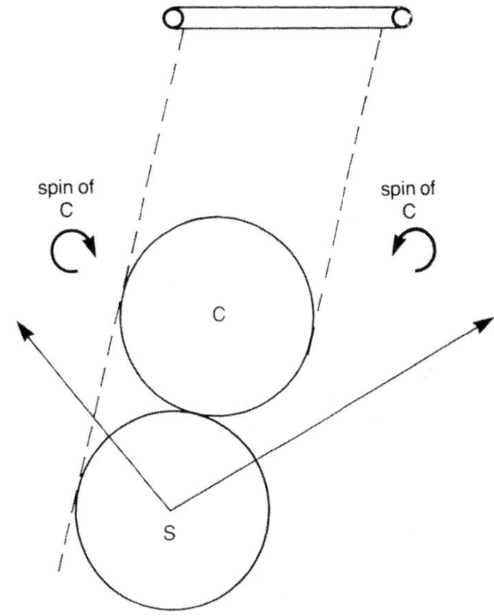

Fig 78 Side spin on the croqueted ball.

same hoop. In this case, you do not need to have a third ball in the vicinity, as the peelee can be roqueted again after the striker's ball has run the hoop. It does usually rule out the possibility of getting a useful rush after running the hoop, or any rush at all if a hoop and roquet is made in the same stroke.

High-bisquers are often addicted to the straight peel when the position occurs fortuitously, when a single hoop and a good rush would make it much easier to set up a break. Remember a successful peel will only give you an extra point, whereas a break could give you half a dozen more.

Provided that the peel is not angled, the closer you are to the hoop, the better. You may even be able to perform the peel so that your own ball comes to rest in the jaws of the hoop but rather more than half-way through. In this case, you will be able to hit the ball to one side with your next stroke to complete the running of the hoop. If the peelee sticks in the jaws of the hoop, you may still be able to complete the peel with a half jump shot as your next stroke.

If the peel is angled, it is better to play the peel with a slight split to leave you with a straight hoop, even though pull may cause problems. It is often difficult to run an angled hoop if the peelee has only just struggled through and impossible to complete the peel with a half jump shot from an angle if the peelee is stuck in the jaws.

The Peel with an Escape Ball (Figs 79–81)

If the two balls are not for the same hoop, then it is necessary to have a third ball that may be roqueted in the vicinity of the peelee's hoop.

Fig 79 The peel with an escape ball.

The third ball is known as the escape or getaway ball. After the peel has been performed, the idea is to rush the escape ball to a useful position, in order to continue the turn with a three-ball break.

The preferred position for the escape ball is slightly to one side of the hoop, so that a straight rush can be played after a split peel. If the escape ball is in front of the hoop, there is a danger that the back swing may be impeded by the hoop after the peel or that the escape ball may impede the back swing on the peeling stroke.

Even if the peel is impossible because of the angle, it may still be worthwhile to play a gentle stroke to leave the peelee in the jaws of the hoop, so that the peel may be completed with a rush later in the turn.

The ideal time to peel a ball is immediately after running the hoop in the opposite direction with your own ball, e.g. to peel 4-back after running hoop 3 or penult after running hoop 6. This is easiest to arrange if the peelee is the pioneer for the hoop; it can then be put in position on the hoop approach. Otherwise, it must be positioned on the approach to the pioneer.

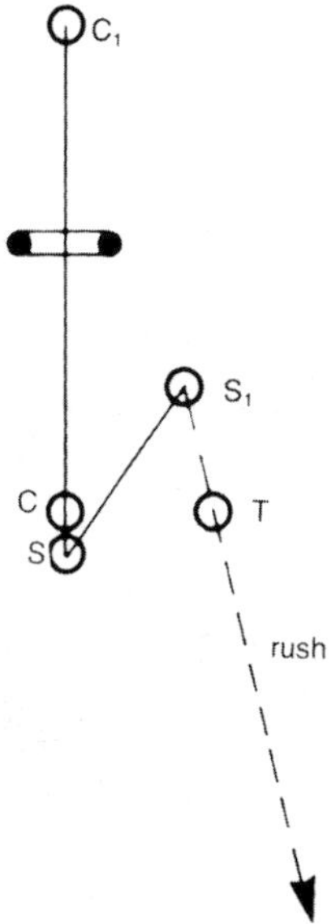

Fig 80 Peel with escape ball.

MISCELLANEOUS SHOTS

The following shots have only one thing in common: they are intended to get you out of a difficult situation – a hampered position. When you are hampered by a hoop, the peg or another ball, special care is required and a referee should be requested to adjudicate the fairness of the shot.

Fig 81 William Prichard stalks the 4-back peel.

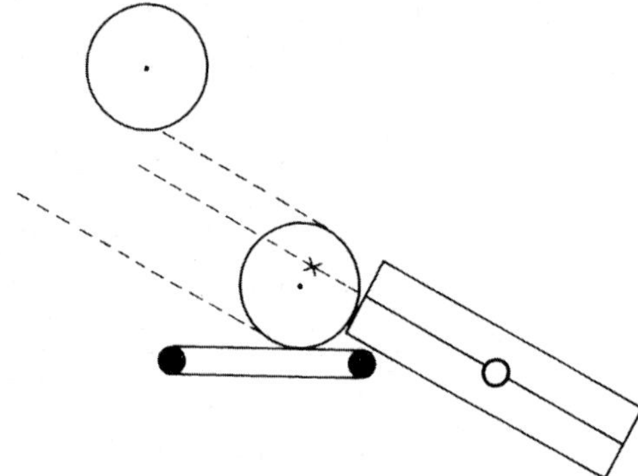

Fig 82 Hampered shot.

Fig 83 A hampered shot.

Hampered Shots *(Figs 82–6)*

A good example of a hampered shot is shown in Fig 82; your red has only just crawled through the hoop and you would like to roquet yellow, which is to the side and in front of the hoop. The shot is possible, as you see when you place your mallet behind the ball, but you cannot hit the ball with the centre of the mallet face. If you swing a little to the left, you will hit the hoop and either fail to hit the ball or your mallet will be deflected so that you will hit the ball with the bevelled edge of the face; a little to the right and you will hit with the bevelled edge. In both cases the result is a fault and the end of your turn.

The response of most players is to restrict their back swing and to stab at the ball with varying degrees of success, but this is quite unnecessary. Your normal swing is the best, but you must concentrate on the line of the swing. The trick is to place your mallet behind the ball and pick a spot on the ball in line with the sight-line on the mallet. Keep your attention focused on this spot, and not on the centre of the ball, and swing gently but normally. An alternative method of playing this shot is to place the mallet head horizontally on the ground behind the ball to be struck and pointing to the target ball. You can then slide the mallet in an arc along the ground to strike the ball.

In Fig 85 red has gone cleanly through the hoop far enough to prevent you playing through the hoop with your mallet but not far enough to give you sufficient back swing. A roll shot action gives you the most powerful shot for a limited back swing, but the hoop is in the way of your normal grip. So, put your mallet in position and put your hand through the hoop to grip the mallet. You will have to crouch down or even kneel on the ground, but you should be able to drive the mallet forward firmly to effect a clean shot.

Fig 84 Keith Aiton experiments with the horizontal technique for a hampered shot.

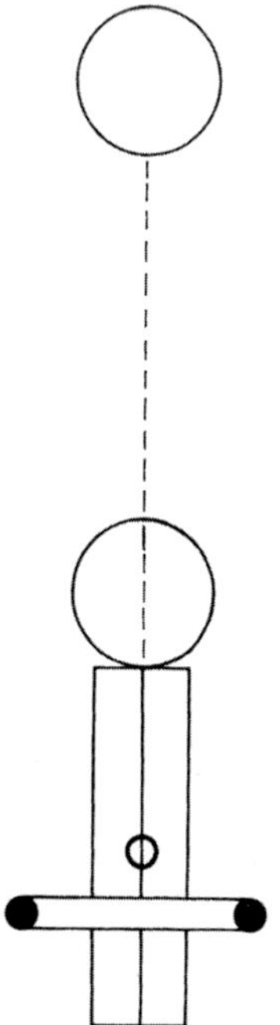

Fig 85 Playing through the loop.

Fig 86 Playing through the hoop.

The Hammer Shot
(Figs 87 and 88)

The hammer shot is an ugly stroke, difficult to execute fairly and one which some would like to see banned. The stroke is played with the player standing in front of the ball with his back to the target ball, hitting downwards at an angle on to his own ball. It is difficult to avoid a double tap or a pull on the ball. Nevertheless, properly played, it can get you out of a tight spot.

In Fig 88 red has rolled awkwardly to the side, so that you cannot swing your mallet back through the hoop, and the wire severely restricts your back swing. To line the shot up, stalk the ball from the opposite direction, stepping over the target ball. You may be able to pick an easily identifiable spot on the grass on the correct line (which you can see when you take your stance) to help your aim; or you can bend over to peer between your legs to see if the mallet shaft is pointing towards the target ball. Some players place the mallet over the top of the ball with the shaft pointing to the target ball to help with the alignment. However, if you do this, you must be careful not to disturb your own ball.

Hit the ball with a smart, angled, downwards blow, trying to whip the mallet head away immediately contact is made. How far up the shaft of the mallet you are able to grip will depend upon the strength of your wrists. If you follow through too far, the result will usually be a horrible scrunch. The shot should sound clean and the ball will invariably jump off the ground due to the reaction from the turf. If it does not, the ball has been trapped between the mallet and ground, and pulled.

Fig 87 The hammer shot.

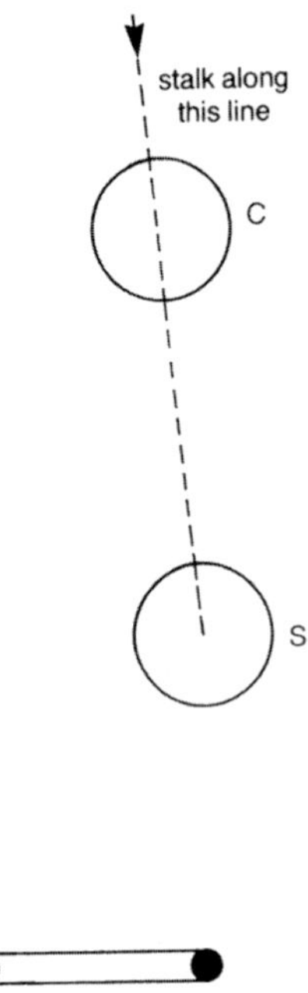

Fig 88 Hammer shot.

The Irish Peel *(Fig 89)*

An Irish peel occurs when both the croqueted ball and the striker's ball are played through a hoop in the same stroke.

The usual situation for the Irish peel occurs when the pioneer has been rushed to an unfortunate position straight in front of the hoop about 6in (15cm) or less on the non-playing side. A take-off past the side of the hoop would leave an uncomfortably angled hoop, particularly if the hoop is on a hill. The solution is to play the Irish peel with a gentle drive, so that yellow finishes about 2ft (60cm) and red about 3in (7.5cm) through the hoop. Then you have a chance to run a controlled hoop with red finishing 3in (7.5cm) through. Of course, you now find yellow on the wrong side of the hoop, so you have to play back through the hoop to roquet it – yes, three times through the hoop to score a point and not break down.

This can also be a useful stroke for a good player faced with a straight double peel to finish the game. In Fig 89 both yellow and red are for penult. Yellow is peeled firmly through the hoop, after taking care to line the balls up so that yellow will not catch a wire and will miss the peg, to a position close to rover; in the same stroke red makes the hoop and can roquet blue.

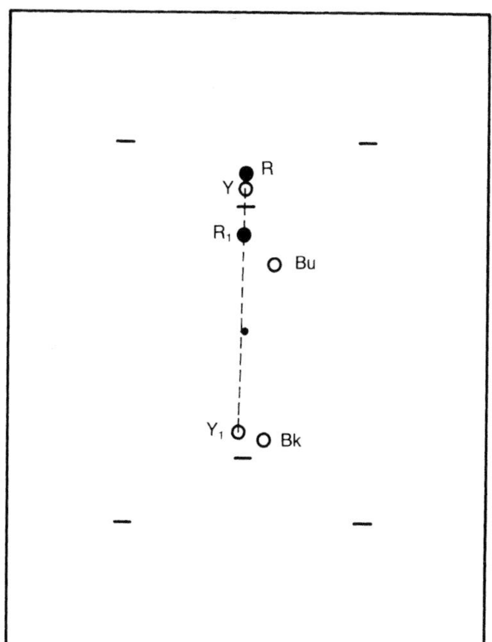

Fig 89 Irish peel at penult.

The Take-Off through the Hoop *(Figs 90 and 91)*

If yellow in Fig 90 is further away than 6in (15cm) but you still do not fancy the take-off round the side of the hoop, you can take off with red through the hoop. This shot requires very careful lining up and can best be done with the aid of your mallet, as shown in Fig 91. Adjust the position of the mallet and striker's ball (red) so that the end face and the tangent to the ball are in line just to miss the near wire. Then play a thin take-off sufficiently firmly for red to run the hoop in the reverse direction.

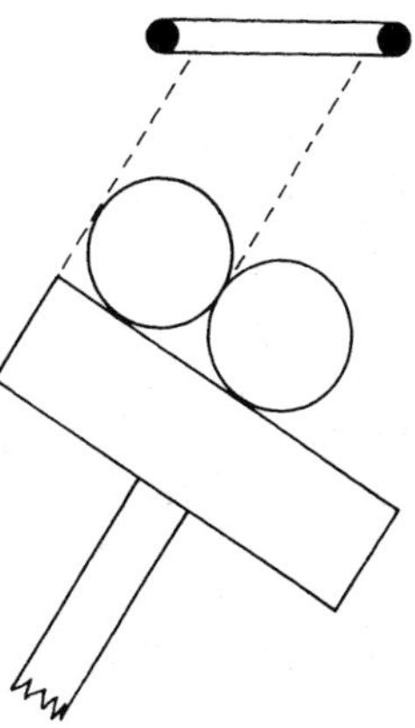

Fig 90 Lining up the take-off through the hoop.

Fig 91(a) Using the end of the mallet to line up a take-off through the hoop.

(b) The view through the hoop.

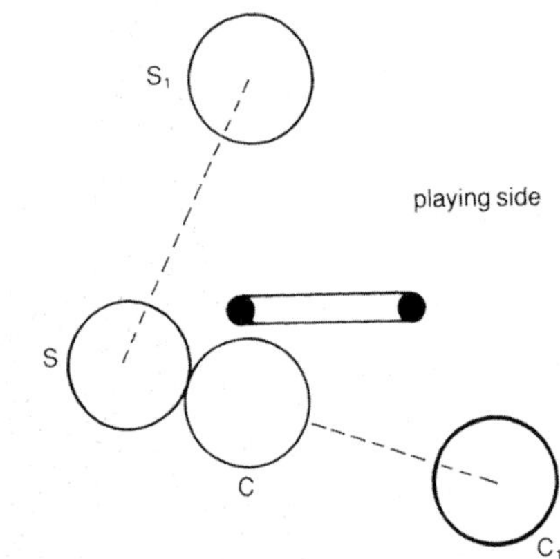

Fig 92 Split away from the hoop.

The Split near the Hoop *(Fig 92)*

You will sometimes find that you have roqueted a ball on to the wire of a hoop on the non-playing side. In this situation there is no problem playing a thin take-off to get to the playing side of the hoop, but to do so would leave the pilot ball impeding the running of the hoop; there is a danger that, on striking the pilot ball, your ball may fail to complete the running of the hoop. The solution is to play a thick take-off or split to put the pilot ball clear of the hoop on the opposite side.

The Thick Take-off in the Jaws *(Figs 93 and 94)*

Occasionally you may find that you have rushed yellow almost into the jaws of the hoop. (Note: if yellow is in the jaws of the hoop, you may take croquet as normal provided that, when the striker's ball has been placed for the croquet, it has not started to run the hoop.) Place red in the jaws of the hoop in contact with yellow and one of the wires (*see* Fig 93). Then play a thick take-off so that yellow is cleared away from the hoop and red bounces back off the far wire into position to run the hoop. This shot should be played without any follow-through and the mallet should be pulled away immediately contact has been made, to prevent red striking the mallet when it rebounds from the far wire.

The Stop Shot into the Jaws *(Fig 95)*

In Fig 95 you need a forward rush after making the hoop, but your rush to the hoop has left yellow too close. Play a split stop shot to send yellow about 2 to 3yd (1.8 to 2.7m) past the hoop and straight in line with it, with red coming to rest in the jaws of the hoop. The wires will take the pace off red and give you a marvellous stop-shot ratio. The shot is easier than it sounds but you have to be confident of your angles. If, by chance, red runs just through the hoop, you will still be able to roquet or even rush yellow by playing through the hoop.

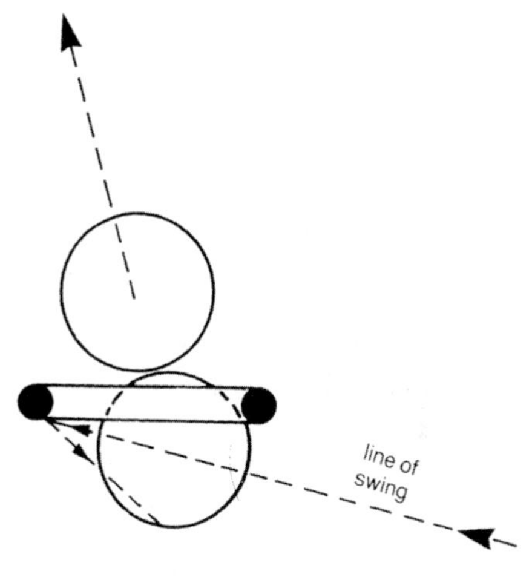

Fig 93 Thick take-off in the jaws.

Fig 94(a) The thick take-off in the jaws: before the stroke.

(b) The result after the stroke.

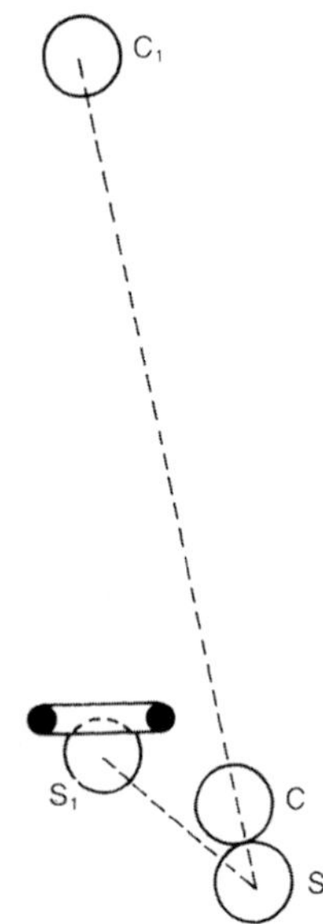

Fig 95 Stop shot in the jaws.

The Jump Shot

The jump shot is played by striking the ball downwards at an angle into the turf and allowing it to rebound. The place where the ball is struck is similar to that for a full or pass roll but the grip is much higher on the mallet and the stance is, therefore, more normal. The mallet should, if possible, be whipped back on impact. It is one of the few strokes in croquet where the right physique is an advantage. It requires a certain amount of strength, and height also helps, if the intention is to jump the ball over a hoop. The shot can be played sideways with a golf-like swing but this is generally to be discouraged. An attempted jump-shot escape from a cross-wired or cross-pegged position (remember that the extension piece can be removed from the peg) is always spectacular but rarely successful.

The shot is always liable to do substantial damage to the turf and is a fault if it does. Jump shots should never be practised on the court; choose a suitable spot at the side of the lawn. The jump shot has the additional advantage that the ball acquires a considerable amount of top-spin and it can be used in a number of situations. A hoop can often be run from an extreme angle with a jump shot. Here the top-spin helps the ball through the hoop should it wriggle in the jaws.

A jump shot can be played to avoid a hoop and roquet in the same stroke, or a half-jump shot can be played to peel a ball through a hoop and run the hoop in the same stroke. In the former case it is worth practising gentle jump shots so that your ball just hops over the other ball.

5 Break Play

Playing a Break

The quickest way to make progress in a game of croquet is to make a break, i.e. in one turn run a number of hoops in the correct sequence. Once the break has been established, the pattern of play is fairly standard and not too difficult to maintain. The breaks are defined according to the number of balls used between running one hoop and the next.

The order of difficulty runs inversely to the number of balls used. A four-ball break is easier than a three-ball break, and a three-ball break is easier than a two-ball break. Good players will seek not only to maintain a break but also to convert it upwards into an easier one.

The Four-ball Break

(Figs 96–9)

The arrangement for a four-ball break starting from hoop 1 is shown in Fig 96. We assume that the striker's ball is red. The colours of the other balls are completely interchangeable, but here we assume yellow is by hoop 1, blue is by hoop 2 and black

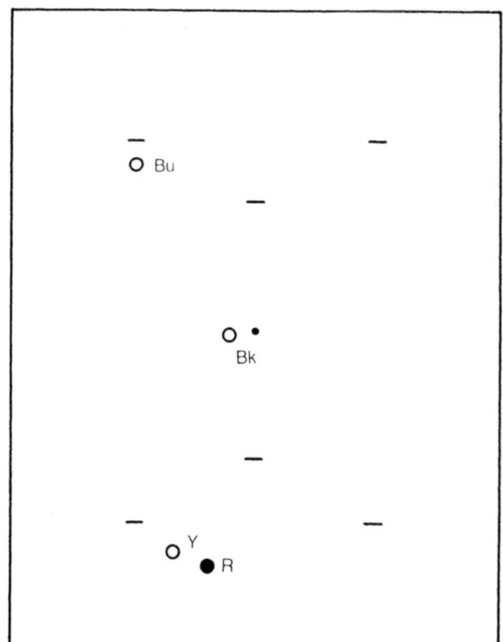

Fig 96 Four-ball break: initial position.

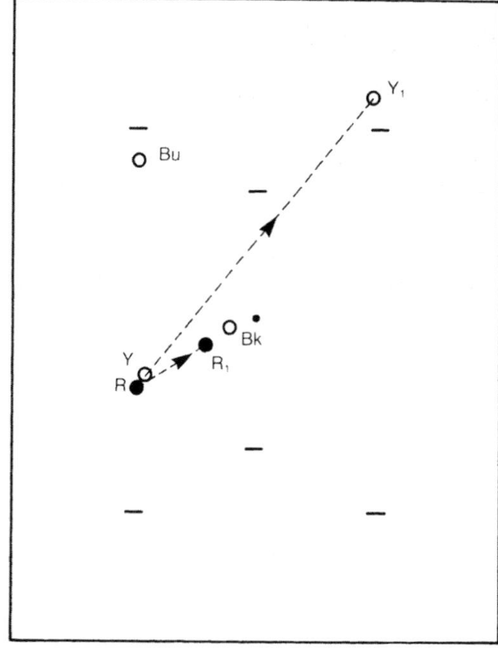

Fig 97 Four-ball break: putting the pioneer to hoop 3.

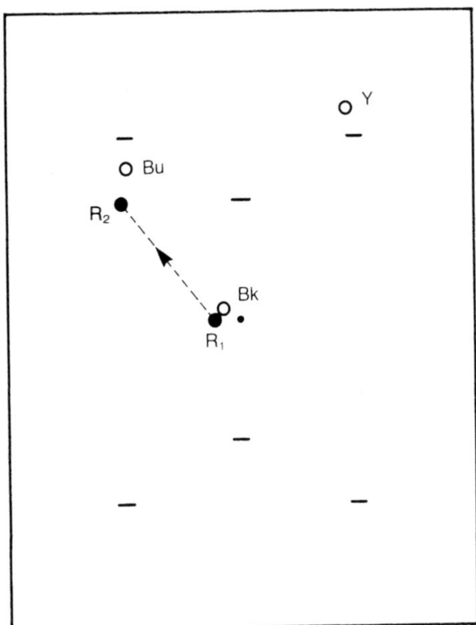

Fig 98 Four-ball break: take-off to pioneer at hoop 2.

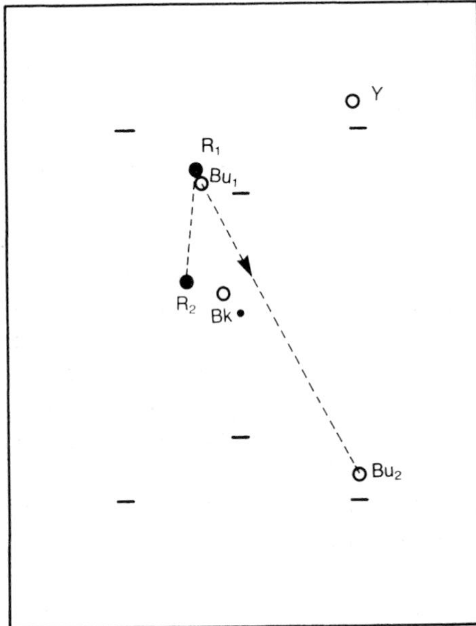

Fig 99 Four-ball break: putting the pioneer to hoop 4.

is by the peg. The balls by hoops 1 and 2 are known as pioneers and the ball by the peg is known as a pivot.

The essential features of the four-ball break are the pivot ball and the pioneers at the next hoop and the next hoop but one. During the course of the break yellow and blue will become pioneers at alternate hoops but black will always remain as the pivot.

Seven strokes are required in progressing from one hoop to the next. These are:

1. Red roquets yellow to a position close to the next hoop (in this case hoop 1).
2. Red takes croquet from yellow with a hoop approach, putting yellow to the far side of the hoop and leaving red in position to run the hoop.
3. Red runs the hoop (once red has run the hoop it is entitled to roquet each of the three other balls once again).
4. Red roquets yellow again, preferably rushing it a little way towards the peg.
5. Red takes croquet from yellow putting yellow as the pioneer at what is now the next hoop but one, i.e. hoop 3 and leaving red conveniently close to the pivot, black.
6. Red roquets black.
7. Red takes off from black to a position close to blue, leaving black by the peg.

At this stage the cycle is complete and examination of the position of the balls will reveal that the essential features are still intact, i.e. there are pioneers at the next hoop and the next hoop but one (hoops 2 and 3), and there is a pivot by the peg.

From here the above sequence of strokes is repeated, except of course that blue and yellow have changed places as pioneers at the next hoop and the next hoop but one. If you are not too familiar with the four-ball break, bear in mind that as soon as you have run a hoop the next croquet stroke should place a pioneer at what is now the next hoop but one, leaving your ball by the peg, and you will not go far wrong.

Placement of Pioneers (Fig 100)

The secret of playing a tidy and well-controlled four-ball break lies in the placement of the pioneers. The ideal position for a pioneer is approximately 1yd (91cm) in front of the hoop on the playing side. (Note: some coaches recommend that beginners should try to place the pioneers at the corners of a rectangle 1yd (91cm) inside the positions of the hoop, on the grounds that the length of the take-off from the peg is reduced; however, then the pioneer has to be rushed into position on the playing side of the hoop. In my experience of coaching beginners, they have fewer problems with the take-off than with the rush.)

The pioneer is placed, of course, with a croquet stroke and it helps if this croquet stroke can be made as easy as possible. Hence the advice in stroke four of the sequence to rush the previous pioneer a little way towards the peg; the new pioneer can then be placed more accurately with a shorter drive or stop shot instead of the more difficult long half-roll. Even worse is to run the first hoop too hard and roquet yellow back towards the south boundary. Not only does this give a longer croquet shot but you may also find that hoop 1, the peg and the pivot are in the way!

If a pioneer is badly placed, the break can be rescued by playing a split shot at no. 7 to put the pivot as a better pioneer or, if this is not possible, playing a split to put the pivot close to the poor pioneer. With the first option, the initial pioneer and pivot are in effect interchanged; with the second option, you should be able to arrange a dolly rush to the hoop with two balls close together.

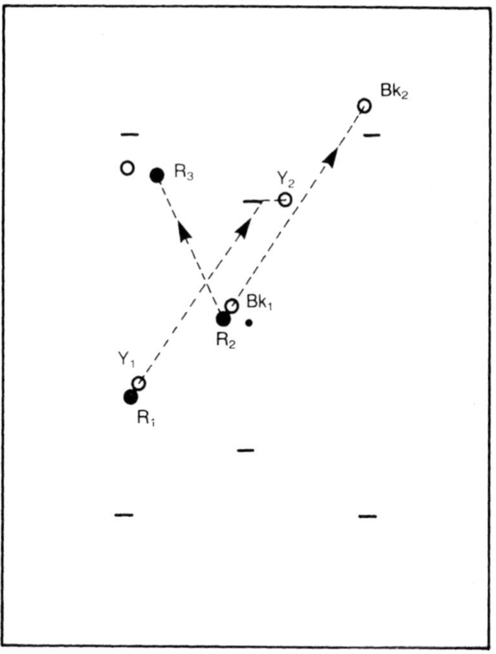

Fig 100 Rescue the four-ball break: the intended pioneer for hoop 3 has hit hoop 6; the pivot is sent as pioneer to hoop 3 instead.

You may find at times that you have rushed a ball too close to the pivot. Your choice is then between (a) placing that ball as a good pioneer at the next hoop but one with a roquet back to the pivot and a longish take-off to the pioneer at the next hoop or (b) leaving the first ball as a new pivot and rushing the original pivot to a position where it can be croqueted as the pioneer at the next hoop but one. You must choose which way to play according to the strengths of your game; are you better at the take-off or the rush? At all costs you must avoid falling between two stools by failing to get a good pioneer or a rush.

You may be tempted sometimes, if you find yourself with a dolly rush on the pilot, to rush that ball as a pioneer to the next hoop but one. The temptation should be resisted;

it is all too easy to underhit or overhit a rush, or cut it off the line completely. Try always to place your pioneers with croquet strokes.

Refining the Four-ball Break (Figs 101 and 102)

It will not always be possible to get a useful rush after running a hoop. One refinement to the standard four-ball break which still makes it possible to play a drive or stop shot for the next croquet stroke is to use a mobile pivot. That is, instead of leaving the pivot in the vicinity of the peg, the pivot is manoeuvred around a rectangle so that it is always within reach of the striker's ball if a drive or stop shot is played.

After the croquet stroke placing the pioneer in position, the pivot is rushed to its next position on the rectangle. This has the additional advantage that the length of the take-off to the next pioneer is reduced. If the pioneer is out of position so that a rush is required to get it close to the hoop, it helps if the pivot can itself be rushed towards the rush line for the pioneer or close to the pioneer to make the subsequent take-off as easy as possible.

You will often see good players apparently knocking the pivot all over the place. They are usually rushing the pivot into such a position that they can play an easy croquet stroke to put the pivot back in position and get on to the pioneer from a short distance rather than play a long take-off.

Whilst all of these refinements are advantageous for the good players, it does demand a high standard of accuracy in both rushes and croquet strokes: high-bisquers are recommended to stay with the standard

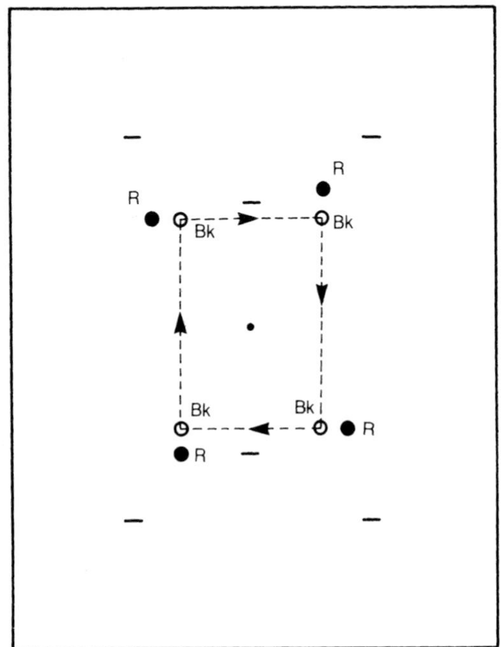

Fig 101 Mobile pivot.

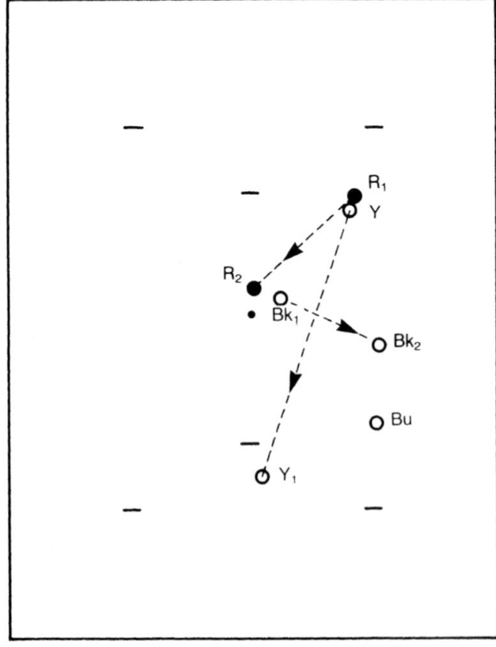

Fig 102 Putting the pivot on the rush line.

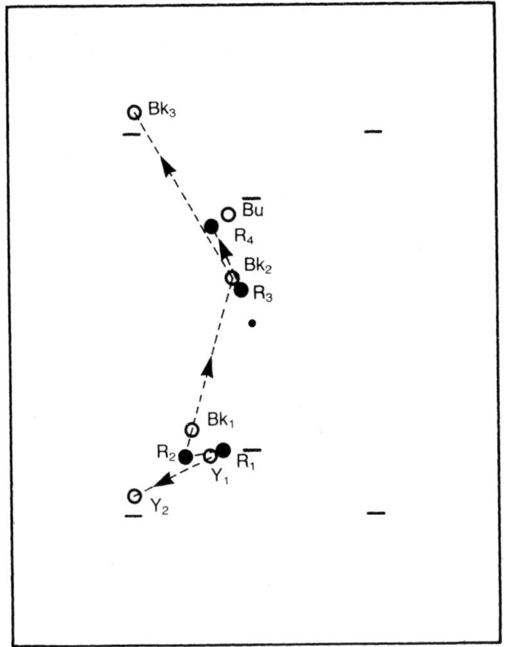

Fig 103 The early pioneer at 2-back

four-ball break until they have acquired sufficient skill in the requisite strokes.

Early Pioneers (Figs 103 and 104)

Experts will often put a pioneer in position at 2-back after making hoop 5, instead of putting the pioneer to 1-back, particularly when taking their first ball round in advanced play. The pivot, which has been taken up close to hoop 5, is rushed near the pioneer at hoop 6 and then croqueted as a pioneer to 1-back. The reason for this line of play is that a very good pioneer is needed at 2-back, because a ball will often be left behind after 1-back in preparation for the leave, and a three-ball break will be played from 1-back to 3-back. As a lift ensues after running 1-back, it is disastrous to break down at 2-back.

Lesser players often imitate this play but are liable to come to grief because they do not take sufficient care over the preparation. It is advisable to have a good pioneer at hoop 6 in the quadrant to the south-west of the hoop. If the pioneer is to the east of hoop 6, the intended pioneer for 1-back will have to be positioned from further away and you may find that hoop 6 or the pioneer at hoop 6 are in the way!

One way of getting a good pioneer at hoop 6 is to put it in this position itself as an early pioneer after making hoop 3. However, the break is often not under complete control at this stage and the early pioneer at hoop 6 is less frequent than that at 2-back.

Some players misguidedly put the early pioneer to 2-back after making hoop 4. This can lead to considerable difficulties if hoop

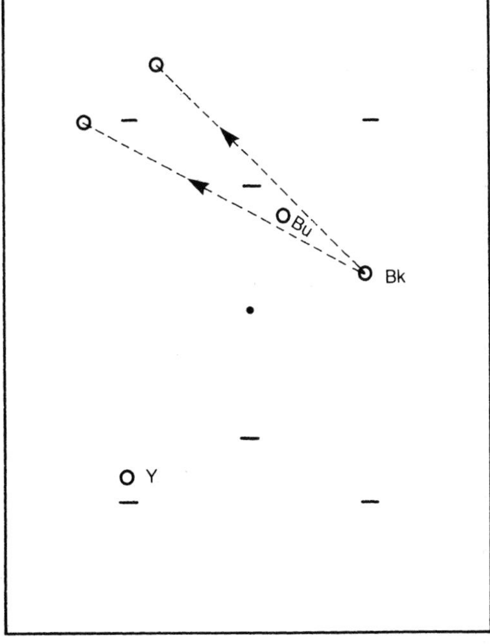

Fig 104 A poor pioneer at hoop 6 and a careless rush after placing the early pioneer at 2-back can lead to a poor pioneer at 1-back.

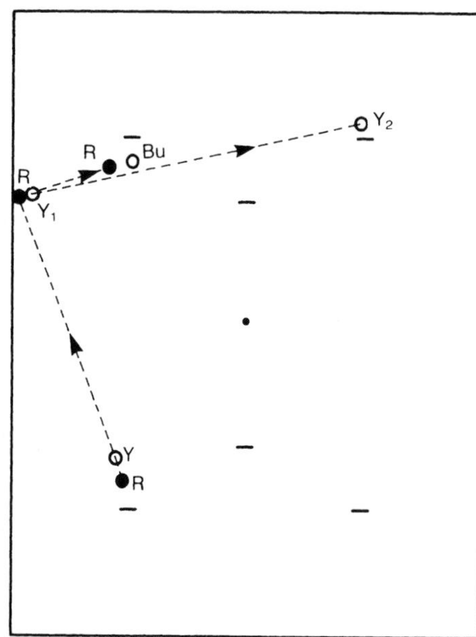

Fig 105 Three-ball break.

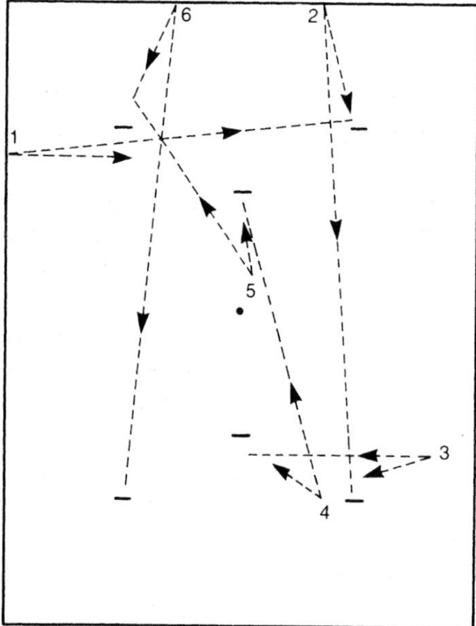

Fig 106 Ideal three-ball break: numbers indicate where the pilot should be rushed to after making a hoop.

5 is run without control and has nothing to recommend it.

Early pioneers are best left to good players in advanced play. There is no necessity for them in handicap play. Indeed, it would be disastrous to break down at hoop 6 with your opponent at hoop 1!

The Three-ball Break

(Figs 105–8)

In terms of the number of shots played to progress from one hoop to the next, the three-ball break is apparently simpler than a four-ball break. However, some of the shots can be a lot more difficult, particularly if the break runs into trouble.

For the purposes of the following discussion of the three-ball break starting at hoop 1, we shall assume that red is still the striker's ball, yellow is the pioneer at hoop 1 and blue is the pioneer at hoop 2. The sequence of strokes is as follows:

1. Red roquets yellow.
2. Red approaches hoop 1 off yellow, putting yellow to the other side of the hoop.
3. Red runs hoop 1.
4. Red roquets yellow.
5. Red takes croquet from yellow, putting yellow as a pioneer to hoop 3 and sending red to blue at hoop 2.

The cycle is then complete and the sequence is repeated with the blue ball instead of yellow, finally sending blue to hoop 4 and red to hoop 3 with the fifth stroke of the sequence. As with the four-ball break, yellow and blue are placed alternately as pioneers.

You will have realised that, so far, I have not said anything about the type of shot required for any of the strokes. If you suppose that the break is to be as easy as possible you can consider the shots in reverse order. Where should the yellow be if you want to play the easiest croquet stroke for stroke no. 5? The answer is, of course, on the west boundary or just in from the west boundary in the vicinity of hoop 2, where you can play a straight drive or stop shot.

How do you get yellow to the west boundary? Clearly, you have to rush it there with stroke no. 4. This means that yellow must be to the west of hoop 1 and sufficiently far north of it, so that you can get a dolly rush after running the hoop. Red must be played into position with a controlled hoop-running shot at stroke no. 3 and yellow must be placed accurately at stroke no. 2. Finally, if you are to have a good chance of getting red close to the hoop and yellow in position at stroke no. 2, yellow must be roqueted into a good position at stroke no. 1 – not too close to the hoop and a little to one side.

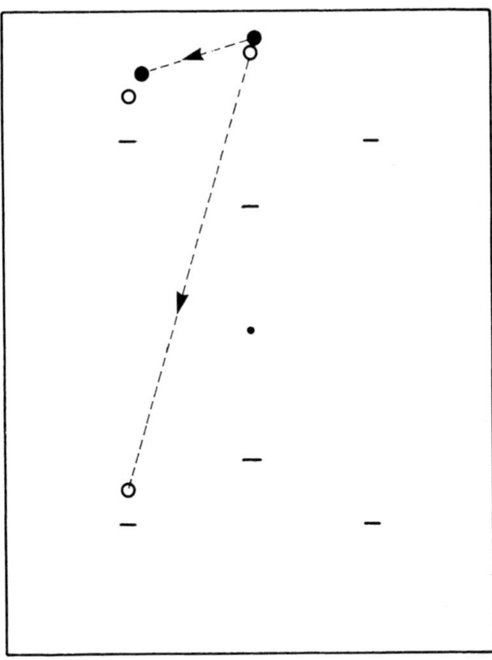

Fig 108 Deep pioneer at 1-back: leave room for the split; the stop shot from the normal position north of 1-back has an impossible ratio.

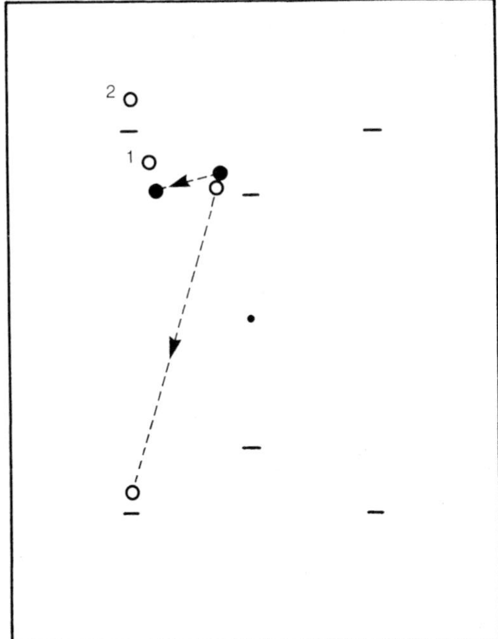

Fig 107 Pioneer south of 1-back (position 1): the split to position 2 is impossible.

None of these shots is difficult but they must all be played well and you must be thinking well ahead. (Note: the preparation for stroke no. 5 actually starts with stroke no. 1.)

Now, think for yourself how to play the break from hoop 2 to 1-back and then compare with Fig. 106. That, of course, is the easy way to play a three-ball break! But what happens when things start to get out of control? Suppose, for example, that you do not get a rush at stroke no. 4. Then you will have to play the big split to hoops 3 and 2 at stroke no. 5 and this is a much more difficult shot than the straight drive. Never mind, remember that this was one of the strokes to practise, on page 46.

Note that you should always plan to put the pioneer into position with a croquet stroke at stroke no. 5. Never plan to put the pioneer in position with a rush at stroke no. 4. Even if you have a dolly rush it is still better, in general, to ignore it. After all, you might finish in a position where it is impossible to play a croquet stroke to give a pioneer at your next hoop but one and, at the same time, get close to the pioneer at your next hoop.

One particular area of difficulty for the three-ball break occurs between hoops 6 and 1-back. If you fail to get a forward rush to the north boundary after hoop 6, you will find it impossible to get a pioneer to 2-back and at the same time get close to the pioneer at 1-back in position 2 (*see* Fig 107). A safety play in this situation, which can occur if the pioneer at hoop 6 is rather loose, is to place the pioneer at 1-back 1 or 2yd (91cm or 1.8m) to the south of the hoop (position 1). This will give you a greater margin of error in the running of hoop 6.

If, on the other hand, you have inadvertently placed the pioneer too deep at 1-back, give yourself room to play a split croquet stroke from the north boundary, rather than trying to rush the pilot behind the deep pioneer (*see* Fig 108).

The Two-ball Break

Only the best players can sustain a two-ball break for more than a few hoops, demanding as it does excellent hoop approaches, controlled hoop running and accurate rushing.

Assume again that red is the striker's ball and the partner ball, yellow, is the second ball. From hoop 1 the stroke sequence is as follows:

1. Red roquets yellow.
2. Red takes croquet from yellow, approaching the hoop and sending yellow to the non-playing side.
3. Red runs the hoop.
4. Red rushes yellow to the next hoop.

At hoop 1 the hoop approach must send yellow 3 to 4yd (2.7 to 3.6m) past the hoop and straight in front of it, so that a controlled hoop-running shot will leave a straight rush to hoop 2. At hoop 2 a sideways rush is required to hoop 3, etc.

It is almost impossible to rescue a two-ball break once it gets out of control, particularly on the outer hoops. If you do not get the rush, you are left with an enormous roll approach to the next hoop with little chance of a rush to the following hoop. In this case, expert players will often approach the hoop with a big split, putting the pilot well down the court, in the hope of running the hoop firmly and making the following roquet.

Converting a Three-ball Break to a Four-Ball Break *(Figs 109 and 110)*

As a four-ball break is easier to play than a three-ball break, the fourth ball should be brought into play at the earliest opportunity. If the fourth ball is already some distance in court, it will usually be best to try to get a rush behind it after making a hoop. The fourth ball is treated as a misplaced pivot by playing a croquet shot after the rush to send the croqueted ball as a pioneer to the next hoop but one, and then rushing the pivot towards the peg. If there is not sufficient room to make this play, the croqueted ball should be sent to the peg and the fourth ball rushed to a position where it can be croqueted to the next hoop but one.

The situation is a little more difficult if the fourth ball is in a corner or on a yard-line. In Fig 109, the fourth ball (black) is in the fourth corner. There is no hope of getting it into play quickly, so bide your time and play the three-ball break as far as hoop 3. Try to get the rush after hoop 3 between hoop 4 and the peg and then take off to the corner ball. This ball can be split to hoop 5 with your ball going to the pioneer at hoop 4. Even if you do not get the rush after hoop 3, you can still play the take-off to the corner ball and carry on from there.

The general principle is to bring out the corner ball with a croquet stroke which sends your ball to the pioneer at the hoop closest to the corner. It helps in this situation if the pioneer for the hoop is a little deep on the non-playing side.

When the fourth ball is on a yard-line, as in Fig 110(a), there will be more opportunities to get it into play. For example, you could try

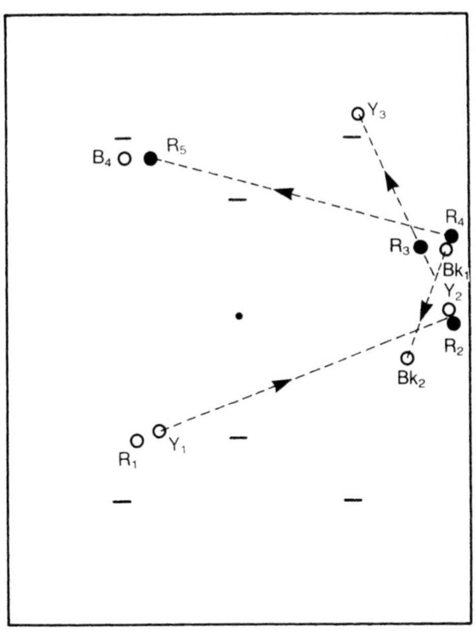

Fig 110(a) Picking up the fourth ball from the east boundary; after hoop 1.

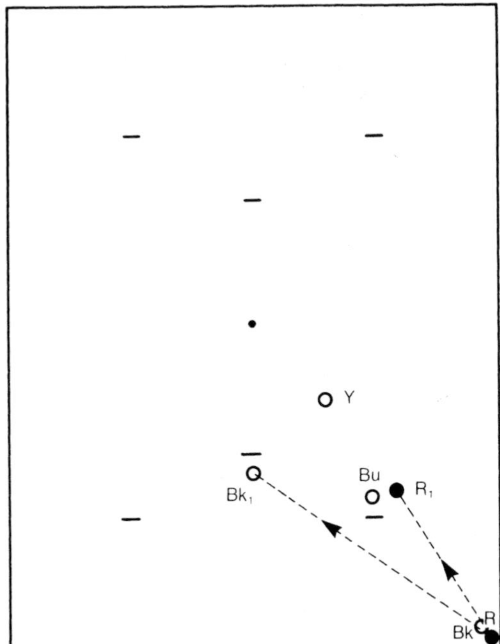

Fig 109 Extracting a ball from the fourth corner before making hoop 4.

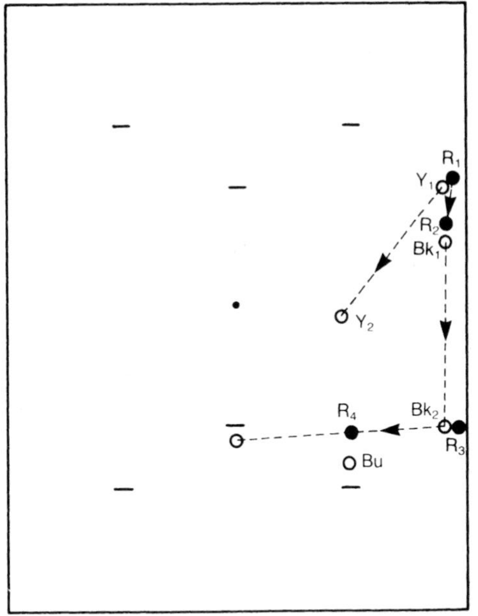

Fig 110(b) After hoop 3.

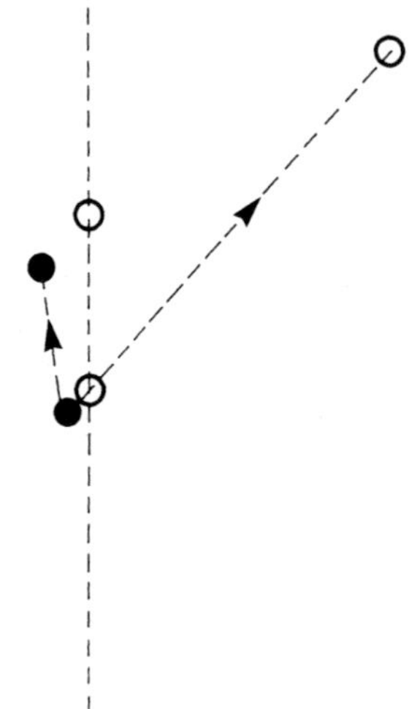

Fig 111 Bringing a ball off the yard-line.

for the rush after hoop 1 to the east boundary and then play the croquet stroke sending the croqueted ball as a pioneer to hoop 3, with your ball finishing close to the fourth ball. If you are confident with your croquet strokes, you might be tempted to try to get behind the yard-line ball and rush it out into court, but this would be rather risky and unnecessary. Play safe, be content to roquet the yard-line ball and then play a thick take-off to the pioneer at hoop 2, bringing the fourth ball into court. Even this play is risky, though, because it is a long way to rush after hoop 1 and it could go wrong, leaving the rushed ball in a position where it is impossible to croquet it as a pioneer and remain close to the yard-line ball.

A quieter play is to continue the three-ball break as far as hoop 3 and try for the rush after hoop 3 to a position on the boundary a couple of yards north of the fourth ball. Then play a little split croquet shot to bring the croqueted ball into court and leaving yourself with a rush on the fourth ball along the boundary, where it can be croqueted to hoop 5. This is a safer play altogether, because the rush after hoop 3 is much shorter than the rush after hoop 1, and the remaining shots are also short ones.

Converting a Two-ball Break to a Three-ball Break *(Fig 111)*

There is a general principle of break play – never leave a ball on a yard-line by playing a thin take-off, even if you need a rush on another yard-line ball. A split stop shot or a thick take-off will bring the croqueted ball out into court and make it so much easier to incorporate that ball later in the break.

This principle is employed in the conversion of a two-ball break to a three-ball break. The idea is to rush the second ball, after making a hoop towards a yard-line ball, in order to get a rush on the yard-line ball and bring the second ball out into court with the croquet stroke. After the next hoop, rush the third ball back towards the second ball, and so on, until you have the second and third balls out under control.

Your best chance of extracting a third ball from a corner is to wait until you reach the hoop adjacent to that corner. If you are good at the split approach from the corner, sending the corner ball to the next hoop but one, it will give you an immediate three-ball break. Otherwise, you can run the hoop and try to get a rush into the corner for a wafer cannon.

6 Tactics

OPENINGS

If you win the toss, what do you do next? You have the choice of playing first or second, or even of deciding which colour balls to play with. If you choose the balls, it does avoid the difficulty of choice of playing first or second, but you may be turning down a slight advantage.

By going in second you will be able to choose the length of the tice. By going in first you will be able to choose whether to attack or defend. Against a weaker player it is probably better to go in first; against a stronger player, second; but the difference is marginal. (For a discussion of the opening in handicap play *see* Chapter 7.)

In the following discussion of the standard opening and its variations it is assumed that red is the first ball played on to the court by Ray, followed by blue played by Bab. (Ray – **R**ed **A**nd **Y**ellow; Bab – **B**lue **A**nd **B**lack.)

The Tice Opening

Red is played to the east boundary to a point between hoop 4 and fourth corner. Blue is played from A baulk to the west boundary, leaving a tice of length 6 to 12yd (5.5 to 11m) according to Bab's assessment of the accuracy of Ray's shooting. Ray now has the choice of shooting at the tice or ignoring it.

Tice Ignored (Figs 112 and 113)

Ray plays yellow to the east boundary to join up with red. The width of the join will depend upon Ray's assessment of the probability of Bab hitting the tice with black; the greater the probability, the wider the join.

1. Bab hits blue with black – she takes off to yellow and splits yellow out into court towards hoop 4, leaving a rush on red to hoop 1. Hoop 1 is made off red, leaving a rush on red to the east boundary towards corner 4. Red is croqueted to hoop 3, leaving a rush on yellow to blue. Blue is rushed to hoop 2, setting up a three-ball break which can easily be converted to a four-ball break.
2. Bab misses blue with black – Bab should play black hard enough to finish in

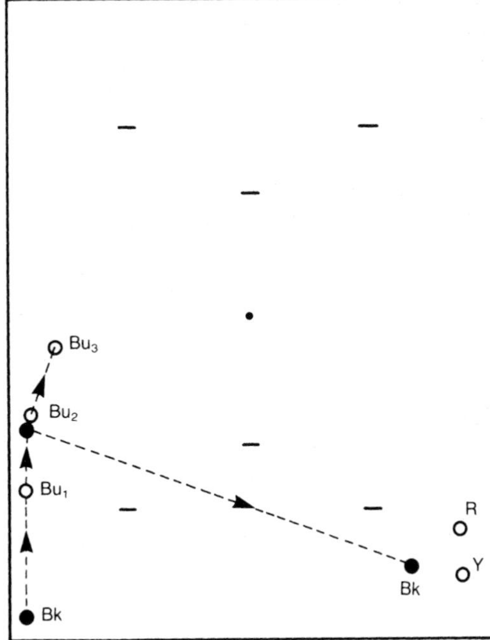

Fig 112(a) Building the break after hitting the tice on fourth turn.

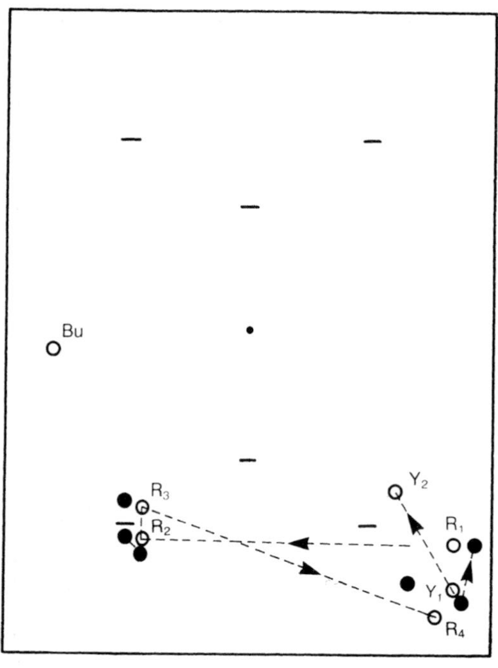

(b)

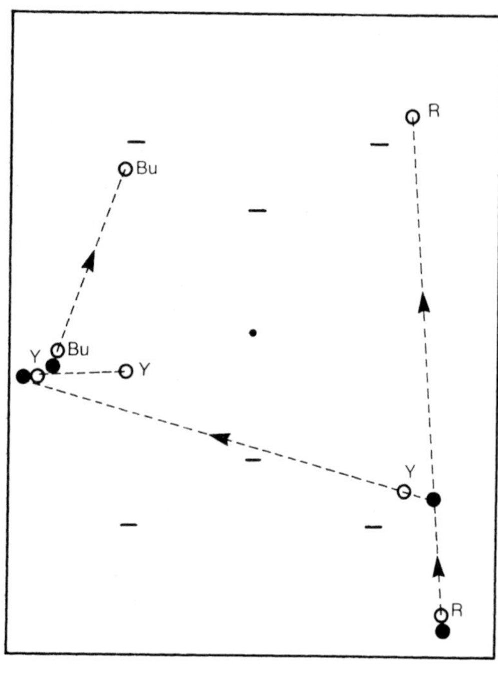

(c)

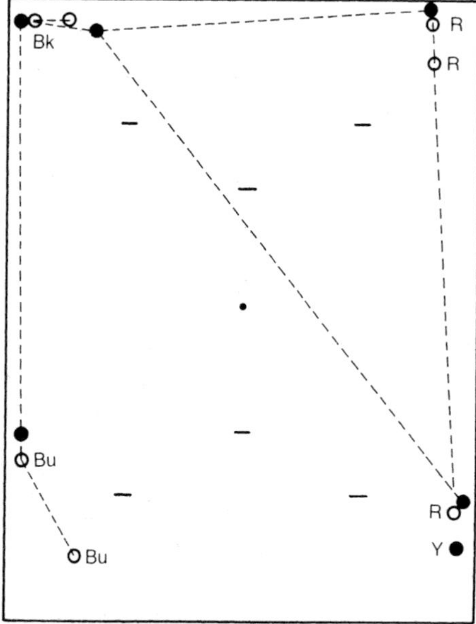

Fig 113 Fifth turn continuation after fourth turn missed shot at the tice.

second corner. If the join is not too wide, Ray can rush red to the north boundary with yellow, take off to black and try to get a rush on blue towards the first hoop. If the join is too wide to attempt the rush safely, Ray should roquet red gently and take off to black, sending red a yard out into court. A slightly thicker take-off to blue will remove black from the corner. If blue cannot be rushed to hoop 1, another slightly thick take-off back to red will bring blue out from the boundary line. Finally, yellow is played to leave a rush on red to hoop 1 or to blue or black. Alternatively, a roll or pass-roll approach to hoop 1 could be attempted but, should it fail, it would be difficult and possibly dangerous in view of the position of blue to leave a rush to hoop 1 for Ray's next turn. A less enterprising Ray would merely leave a rush to hoop 1 after roqueting red, leaving black in the corner and blue on the yard-line.

Tice taken (Fig 114)

1. Ray hits the tice with yellow – the usual play is to take off thickly to red, sending blue a few yards towards hoop 2. Red is roqueted and a rush is left to blue from the boundary a little north of hoop 4. There are then good prospects of a three-ball break if black misses the long shot from B baulk or the shorter, but more dangerous, shot from A baulk. An alternative, but more speculative, play is to try for position at hoop 1 with a thick take-off to obtain a two-ball break.
2. Ray misses the tice with yellow – Ray has the choice of shooting hard to finish in corner two or softly to finish 10 to 12yd (9 to 11m) north of blue, threatening a return shot. If yellow is in corner two, Bab should shoot at blue from an angle so that they are joined up if the shot is missed. If the shot is hit, black can try to approach hoop 1 with a split roll, so that blue is sent towards corner one. If the hoop approach fails, it is then easy to retire with a simple rush on blue to hoop 1. If yellow is too close to risk a miss with the angled shot, particularly if yellow has missed on the right, Bab can shoot hard at blue from corner one with black, finishing in corner two if the shot is missed, or play to the west boundary 4yd (3.6m) out from corner one, to guard against yellow's shot.

On balance, it is better for Ray to shoot at the tice, unless it is so long that he has good reason to believe that Bab will miss. A hit for Ray gives him an immediate advantage and a miss leaves no immediate break for Bab, should she hit.

Other Openings

The tice opening is a well-balanced opening, offering opportunities to whichever player hits a shot, with good defensive prospects for either player. Other openings are usually less well balanced and often yield a break as well as the innings to the successful hitter. As such, they are often used as shock tactics against a less experienced player.

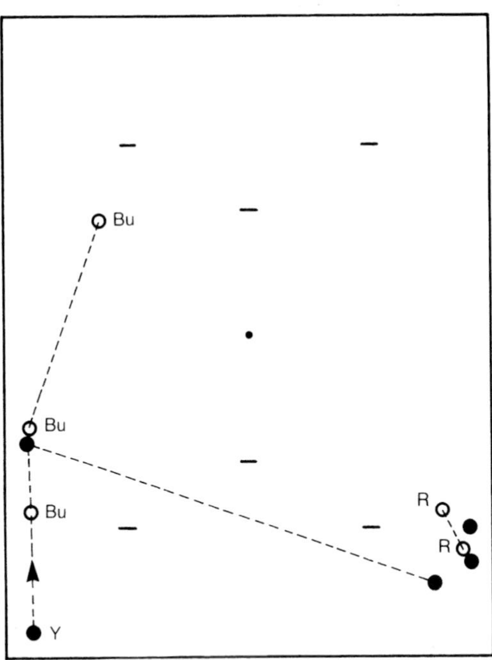

Fig 114 Continuation after third turn hit on the tice.

The Duffer Tice (Fig 115)

This variation of the tice opening is named after Duff Matthews. After Ray has played red to the east boundary, Bab plays blue from the end of B baulk along a line somewhat to the west of hoop 4. The length of the tice can be from 6 to 9yd (5.5 to 8m). It is difficult for Ray to shoot at blue from the end of B baulk, as a miss will leave yellow uncomfortably close to the end of A baulk. A missed shot from any other position on B baulk that does not finish close to A baulk

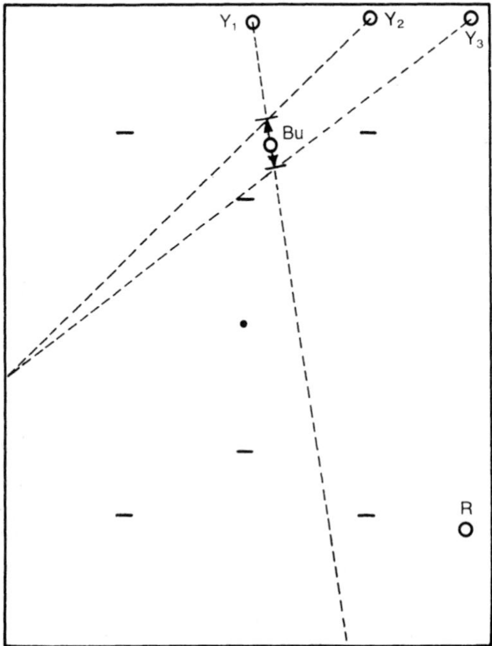

Fig 115 The Duffer tice: Ray cannot afford to miss from Y_1; the shot from Y_2 or Y_3 is longer.

has to be taken from a much greater distance than the simple tice offered. If the tice is short, it cannot be ignored; otherwise the usual counter is a wide join with red.

Bab Shoots at Red on the East Boundary (Figs116 and 117)

This is a tactic often used by a stronger Bab against a weaker Ray. If Bab hits, both balls are rolled towards the peg to leave a double target from either baulk and preferably with red hampered by the peg from eventually taking a short shot at blue. The double is at least 16yd (14.4m) (equivalent to a single ball target at 8yd (7.2m)), and can be longer if the double is from a position more towards the corners.

Ray cannot afford to shoot normally at the double: a missed shot would finish in baulk. A soft shot by yellow will give an immediate advantage if it hits, but will probably leave a juicy triple target if it misses. A better plan for Ray, if he has an open shot at blue with red, is to play yellow to the boundary, so that red can rush blue to yellow. Otherwise, corner two or corner four offers the best defence. Bab, of course, is not inhibited from shooting normally on the fourth turn with black.

If Bab misses on the second turn with blue, Ray should not be tempted to shoot with yellow unless a double target is offered by blue and red. He is much more likely to leave a double target himself with two balls already on the boundary, and the fourteen-yard shot will be missed more often than not by most Babs. If he wants to put press-

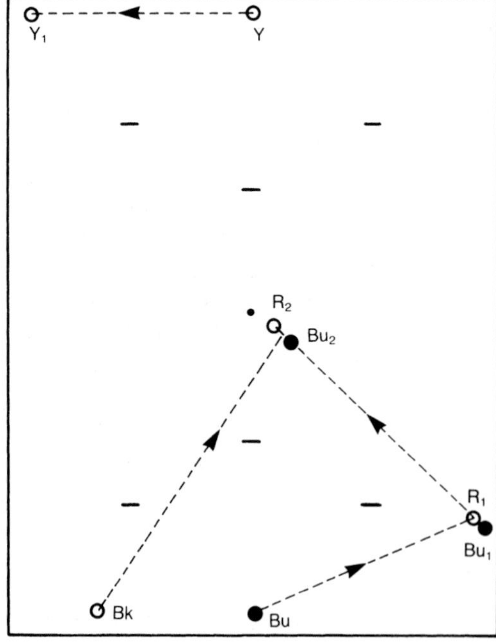

Fig 116 Blue hits red on second turn: Ray cannot afford to miss the double with yellow and is hampered with red on the fifth turn by the peg.

ure on Bab, he should play yellow to the peg. Otherwise, corner two will offer a safer defence against Bab hitting.

An interesting variation for Bab, if she hits, is to play red down the yard-line approximately in line with hoop 3, and then to play blue into the first corner. Ray is then faced with an awkward decision. It is virtually impossible to move red and blue to safe positions if he plays at blue. Similarly, it is impossible to move red to safety with the long take-off to the first corner, unless red has been fortuitously rushed well down the court. It is generally safer for yellow to roquet blue, and then croquet it well down the west yard-line with a drive approach to hoop 1. The approach is somewhat speculative, but Ray can always retreat in safety to corner four with yellow.

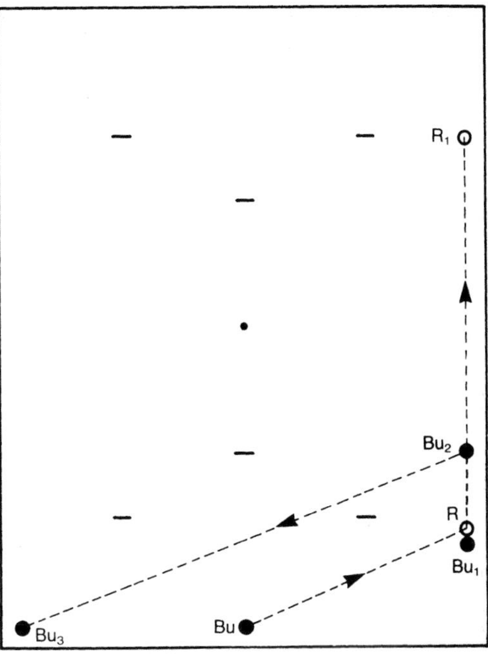

Fig 117 The dilemma: Ray cannot easily move both red and blue to safety.

Red Plays Slightly North of Hoop 1

This is sometimes called the joke opening, but it is not always clear who has the last laugh. The intention is for Ray to join up with blue on the third turn, wherever Bab plays blue on the second turn. Bab can shoot at red to finish in, or near, the second corner if the shot is missed; or leave a tice of about 12yd (11m) on the east boundary from B baulk. In the latter case, yellow cannot join up with blue without leaving an inviting double target. If red is not disturbed, a hit on third or fourth turn will usually get the game away to a quick start.

Red Plays to the Peg

This is another opening which will start the game quickly, if there is a hit on third or fourth turn. If Bab is a good shot, she can play blue to join up with red, leaving a double target. Otherwise, a 12yd (11m) tice on the west boundary from A baulk will make it impossible for yellow to join up with blue. If the tice is hit, it is still quite difficult for Ray to get the three-ball break.

With both of the last two openings, Ray can play red away to safety if nothing is hit on third or fourth turns.

The Corner Two Opening

Bab may decline to set a tice and instead play blue to the west boundary about 6in (15cm) south of corner two. Her intention is to shoot at blue on the fourth turn. Ray cannot afford to shoot at blue on the third turn because there is little to gain if he hits and he will leave a double if he misses. Ray should set a wide join on the east boundary on the third turn in order to minimise the chance of Bab getting the break with a successful shot. If Bab misses, Ray has a much better chance of establishing the break with either a cannon from corner two or at worst a rush to hoop 1.

On balance, the standard tice opening is best; other openings are more of a gamble and are best left to those with an adventurous spirit.

LEAVES

General Principles
(Figs 118 and 119)

Towards the end of any turn when you have the innings, whether you have made a break or not, you must plan to make a good leave, that is, to leave the balls in such positions that are to your advantage and to your opponent's disadvantage. The act of making a leave is known as laying up.

A special category of leaves is necessary for advanced play. For a discussion of these leaves see Chapter 8.

At the start of your turn, you may find that the balls are not in a favourable position for you to try to make a break. Too many players try to make a break on every turn and, in so doing, lose the opportunity to make a good leave. If the balls do not lie favourably, be patient and sort them out so that you have a good chance of making a break on your next turn. In particular, do not bring your partner ball well out into the court unless you are certain that you can make your next hoop: it is not wise to join up too far away from the yard-lines.

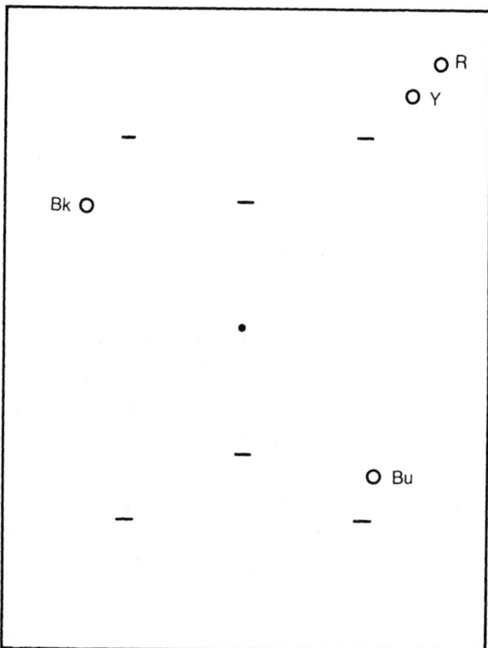

Fig 118 The trap: Red for hoop 3. Bab should move blue but cannot shoot into the trap Ray has laid in the third corner.

The first and obvious principle of a good leave is that you should not leave your opponent an easy shot. This means that his balls must be well separated from each other and from your balls. Be careful, also, that you do not offer your opponent a double target. Bear in mind, however, that if you are responsible for the position of either of his balls, it must not be wired from the other three balls, otherwise he could claim a lift and play from either baulk. Basically, a ball is wired from another ball if it is impossible to play a shot to hit any part of the other ball because a hoop or the peg is in the way or would impede the back swing.

The second principle is to make it dangerous for your opponent to shoot and miss. This is the principle behind the trap, where you lay up 3 or 4yd (2.7 or 3.6m) in from a boundary line. If your opponent shoots and misses, you can turn round, roquet his ball and stop shot it into court, leaving a useful rush on your partner ball. This is also a

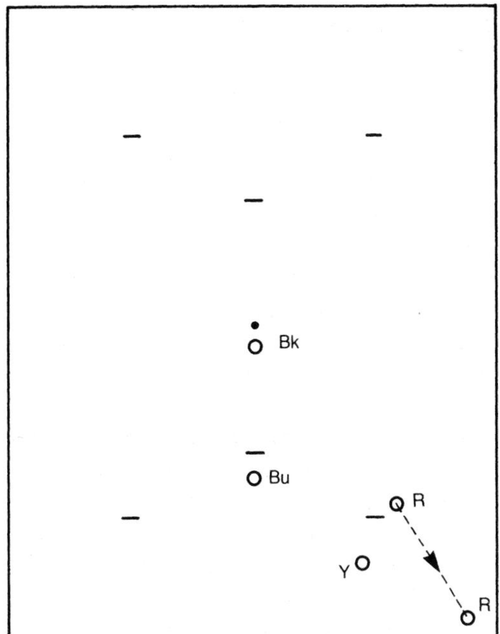

Fig 119 Guarding the boundary: Ray has failed to approach hoop 4 with red.

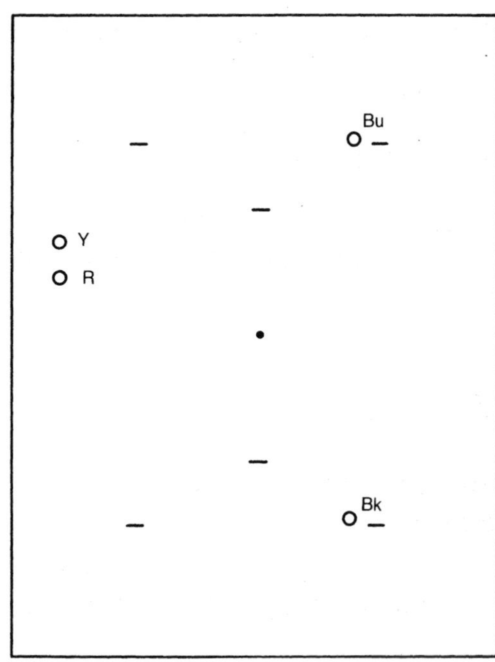

Fig 120 The simple squeeze: red for hoop 3; yellow for hoop 4.

useful principle to adopt if you fail to approach a hoop correctly off your partner ball. You should try to discourage your opponent from shooting at your open ball by guarding the boundary along the line of fire. In Fig 119, having failed to approach hoop 4 successfully, guard the boundary behind yellow. Then, if blue takes the 8yd (7.2m) shot and misses, you can pick up the break again.

The third principle is to leave a position where you can make some progress, even if your opponent plays defensively.

The fourth principle, one that is often overlooked, is not to leave the balls in such positions that your opponent has an easy break if he hits in. In other words, be careful not to leave your balls or his partner ball by his next hoop, and remember that you have to consider this with respect to each of his balls.

It may not always be possible to incorporate all of these principles in the leave; if not, the order of importance is as given.

The Squeeze
(Figs 120 and 121)

The simplest variation of the squeeze occurs when your two balls are for different hoops. You then leave your opponent's balls as pioneers at these hoops as in Fig 120. Whichever ball your opponent plays with will leave you a pioneer. Note also that, if he shoots with black at blue or with blue at black, you can pick up a three-ball break with ease.

In these circumstances there is a strong temptation for your opponent to shoot at one of your balls, on the grounds that he has little to lose. However, if you leave your balls a

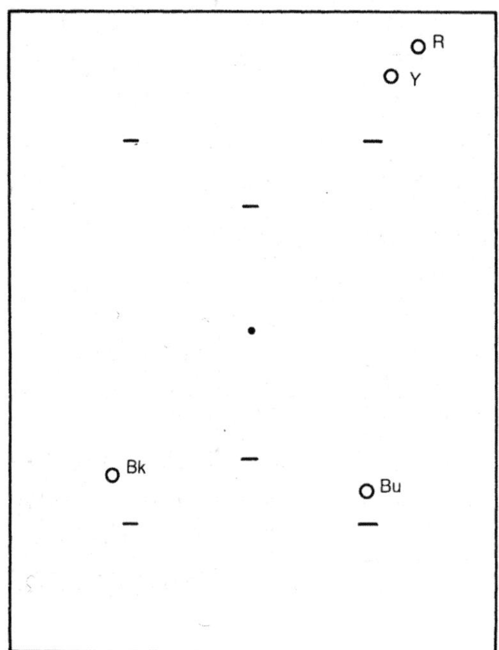

Fig 121 The squeeze with a pioneer and a rush to the fourth ball. Red for hoop 4 and yellow for hoop 5.

couple of yards in from the boundary, you should be able to get his ball well out into court and pick up a three-ball break using your partner ball. If your opponent plays defensively by putting one ball in a corner, you can cut rush to a short boundary and split to get a three-ball break.

It is not always possible to lay a simple squeeze or even advisable to do so. For example, you may be for hoops 4 and 5; to leave pioneers at these hoops would offer your opponent far too short a shot and contravene the first principle. The solution is to leave one of his balls as a pioneer at one hoop and the other 4 or 5yd (3.6 or 4.5m) in from a yard-line with a rush towards it, as in Fig 121. If blue shoots at black, you can rush yellow to the west boundary, play blue to hoop 5 and rush black to hoop 4. If blue is played defensively to a corner, you can still rush yellow to the west boundary and play for the rush on black to hoop 4, but beware of putting yellow to hoop 5 unless you are absolutely confident of making hoop 4 off black.

The Wired Leave *(Figs 122–3)*

One of the most powerful leaves is to arrange your opponent's balls cross-wired at your next hoop and your own balls far away with a useful rush.

Before the introduction of advanced play it was usual amongst experts for the first break to be taken to the peg, leaving the opponent's balls cross-wired at hoop 1 and the player's balls in the third corner. If the opponent missed the shot of some 35yd (31.5m), the game was more or less over.

The preparation for a cross-wire should begin before the last hoop but one that you want to make. In particular, you should arrange that your partner ball is either the pivot or pioneer for this last hoop but one.

Fig 123(a) shows the preparation for a cross-wire at hoop 1. Red has just made penult off yelow and roqueted it again. Yellow is croqueted to hoop 1 with red finishing close to blue. Blue is croqueted close to yellow (clearly, the original positions of blue and yellow were interchangeable) with red finishing close to black. Rover is made off black leaving a rush to hoop 1. Black is croqueted diagonally to hoop 1, and the position of blue is adjusted with a little roquet and croquet, leaving a rush on the partner ball to safety.

Note that the final cross-wire is achieved with a very short, and therefore accurate, croquet stroke. If black has been placed fairly close to the hoop, the margin for error in placing blue is very much increased. The cross-wire is often attempted by less expert

Fig 122 A nicely wired leave.

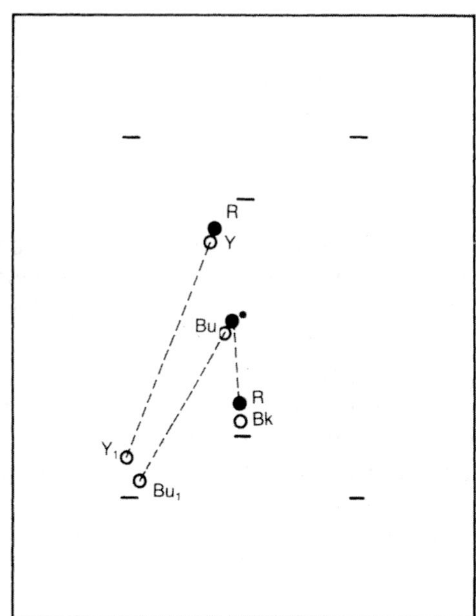

Fig 123(a) The cross-wire at hoop 1: preparation.

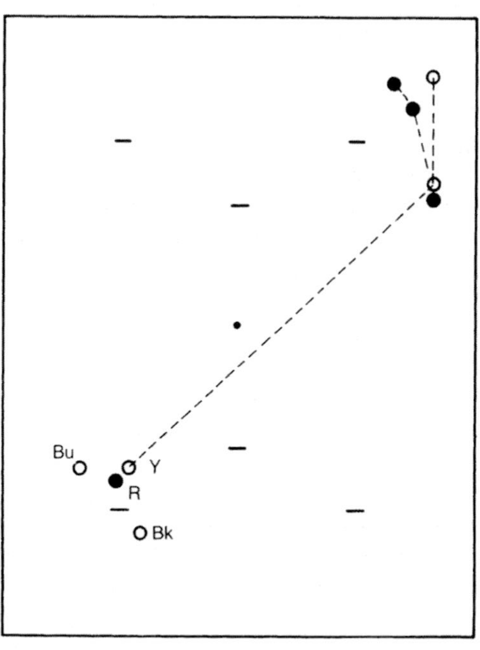

(b) The final stages.

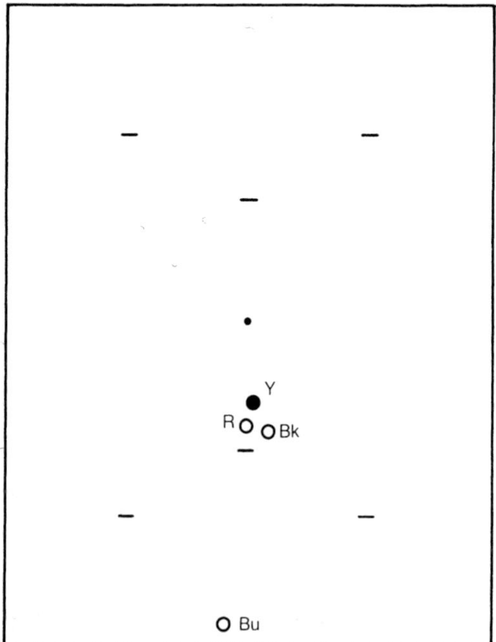

Fig 124 Position for the straight rover peel.

players without the help of the partner ball. The final shot has to be a take-off back to partner and it is very easy to leave the intended cross-wired balls open.

The same procedure can be used for a cross-pegged leave but this is not as easy to achieve successfully as a cross-wired leave.

THE END-GAME

You are happily going round with your second ball on a tidy four-ball break, with your forward ball already for the peg. At this stage you need no help from me. Keep your head and you are home and dry. But there are other situations which are not so clear cut and here technique and tactics can make all the difference between winning and losing.

The Rover Peel
(Figs 124 and 125)

If your forward ball (red) is for rover and you have a four-ball break with yellow, it is not too difficult to finish on that turn, provided, of course, that you think ahead and prepare properly. For example, will red be your pioneer for 3-back? If the answer is yes, it will therefore be your pioneer at penult and it will be difficult to get it into position for the rover peel unless you do something about it.

Fig 124 shows the ideal position of the balls for the straight rover peel. Yellow has croqueted blue to its present position but can still roquet red and black. Forget about black for the moment, roquet red and, with a gentle drive or stop shot, peel it through the hoop. Now roquet black and approach rover off black, putting it a few inches past the hoop and to one side. Run the hoop gently and you will be able to roquet black again and take off to get a rush on red to the peg.

The reason for roqueting red first and not black is to guard against mishaps. If the peel sticks in the jaws, you will be able to try to promote it through with black on the croquet stroke. If the peel takes a little wire and struggles through by a few inches so that it would be impossible to run the hoop without roqueting red, you will have the opportunity to knock it out of the way with black on the hoop approach.

What about the position of blue? Well, if, in spite of all your efforts, red remains too close to the hoop to be able to run the hoop without making the roquet, you can still jump through the hoop and over red to the south boundary close to blue. Or, if red is stuck in the jaws and a promotion is not possible, a half-jump shot will peel it through with yellow going to the boundary.

It is paying attention to these little details

which makes the difference between winning the game on that turn and giving your opponent a last chance.

Now, let us see how to get the balls to the most desirable position. If red is the pioneer for 4-back, you will be able to position red on the croquet stroke after making 4-back. To make this shot as easy as possible, you will be looking for a rush back towards the peg after making 4-back. Technically, it is better to play for the rush on black back behind penult, in order to croquet it into position, finishing close to the pioneer at penult. However, if black is near the correct position already, a little rush and take-off back to the penult pioneer is a justifiable alternative.

If red is the pivot, the play is almost identical: just substitute red for black and vice versa in the previous paragraph. Do be careful, though, not to put black in the jaws of the hoop or straight in front of it. It is surprisingly easy to do if you are not thinking.

If red is the pioneer for 3-back, then red is croqueted into position in front of rover after 3-back, leaving a rush on the pivot – it helps to have the pivot somewhere between rover and 3-back – to the east boundary, where it can be croqueted as the pioneer at penult.

In all of these cases both red and black are put into position before making penult. If red is too much to one side, black may be roqueted first in order to get a dolly rush on red. You forgo the chance of a cannon in favour of cleaning up the position.

Penult is made off blue, and blue is rushed 2 or 3yd (2 or 3m) past the peg on the opposite side of red from black. In that way, black will not get in the way of blue when it is croqueted into position.

Even if things start to go wrong and the peel is not possible, you should still be able

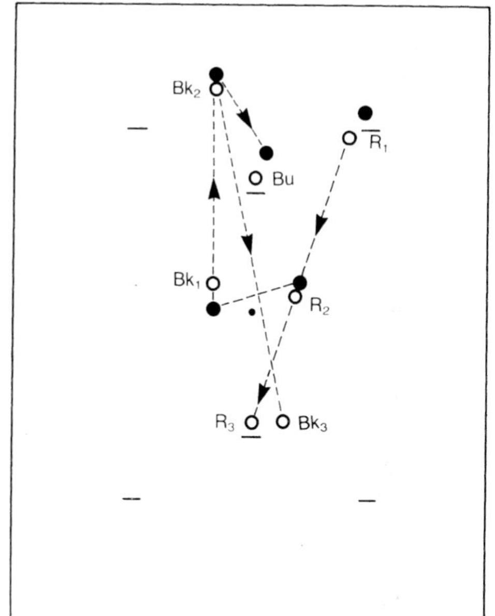

Fig 125(a) Preparation for the straight rover peel: red as pioneer at 4-back.

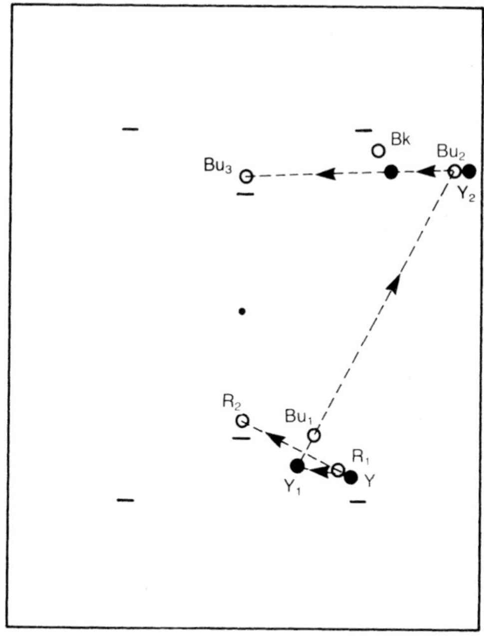

(b) Red as pioneer at 3-back.

to keep control. Just concentrate on completing the turn and making a good peg and rover leave.

The Three-ball Ending

Croquet players are not good spectators: most prefer to play rather than to watch. If you see a group gathered round a lawn, it will usually be to watch a game in which one of the balls has been pegged out.

The Single-Ball Player

If your opponent has pegged out your forward ball, you have three choices at the start of every turn. You can shoot at the opponent's balls, take position for your next hoop or lurk in a menacing position for your opponent.

Sooner or later you will have to hit in, and you may have to do so several times if your ball still has a lot of hoops to make. You should shoot at every opportunity, even if it is a very long shot, provided that you are not shooting into a trap to give away a three-ball break. If you are a long way behind and are presented with a moderate length shot, say 10 to 12yd (9 to 11m), it will probably pay you to shoot, even into the trap, but shoot at the far ball; the difference in the probabilities of hitting at 12yd (11m) as opposed to 10yd (9m) is not so great compared with the enormous advantage of getting both balls out into court early. When you hit in, you must make the most of your opportunity and try to get a three-ball break going.

On most occasions that you do hit in, the opponent will be joined up, so you ought to be able to get a rush on his other ball to your next hoop. If the balls are lying awkwardly and you are for hoop 4 or 5, your best chance of making progress may be a two-ball break round the easier centre hoops. Indeed, if you can play precision rushes, the two-ball break or the rush back to the third ball, gradually working both balls into the open, is the most satisfying play. Otherwise, it is time to throw caution to the winds and play the kind of speculative shots that you would normally avoid, in order to get the break going.

At the very least, if a rush is not possible, you ought to be able to separate your opponent's balls and take position at your next hoop with your final continuation stroke. If this option is forced upon you, try to put the opponent's balls somewhere where you will have a decent shot at one of them, if you run the hoop hard.

If your opponent has been skilful enough to leave a trap and a very long shot for you, it will be time to lurk in position to menace his next hoop or next hoop but one, should he break down. The best position to lurk is one which leaves your ball behind the break if he succeeds in running his next hoop. The corners for the outer four hoops and the side boundaries for the middle two hoops are the best positions. If your opponent has demonstrated his ability to leave you wired from both of his balls without conceding a lift (i.e. he is not responsible for the position of your ball), you might consider the thin-wire position for the outer four hoops, that is, on the side boundary parallel to the hoop where it is very difficult for the opponent to arrange a wired position. However, this is not a good position if your opponent is good at the 6yd (5.5m) roll. Another good time to lurk is when your opponent has broken down and separated; then you may be able to find a position on a boundary equidistant from each of his balls.

Taking position at your next hoop is not usually a good tactic; it leaves your ball out in the open and makes it easier for your opponent to pick up a three-ball break. The exceptions are: (a) when your opponent is not joined up; (b) when your opponent has been successful in keeping you wired from his balls but does not have a rush to his hoop. Then you force him to move your ball and leave you a shot.

Take heart! The single-ball player often wins a three-ball ending.

The Two-Ball Player

There are two basic ways for you to proceed. You can ignore your opponent's ball completely and progress around the court on a two-ball break, being careful at the end of your turn to leave your balls wired from your opponent's ball, particularly so if he is fairly close. However, this requires a high degree of skill and is really only appropriate for a low handicap player. Alternatively, you can try for a three-ball break by leaving a trap for your opponent. Of course, if your opponent does shoot and miss, make the most of your opportunity.

Remember, though, that your opponent will probably shoot if he is close enough, and you certainly do not want him to hit. Paradoxically, you have to leave a trap which discourages him from shooting, because the shot is very long, but one which still gives you a chance to make progress. This is not too difficult for the outer four hoops, because you can lay the trap from the corner adjacent to your next hoop, with a rush to that hoop. The danger area is the path through the middle two hoops. Take no chances with these; if you fail to get position on the rush, retreat with both balls and try again next turn. Above all, do not join up in the middle of the court.

Similarly, if you have left your opponent with a shot of less than 15yd (13.5m) at your partner ball, retire to a distant corner; you can always join up later. The most your opponent is likely to make, whether he hits in or takes position, is one hoop.

You might also consider pegging out your forward ball, if you are well ahead with your backward ball. How far ahead will depend on the standard of your opponent. Perhaps, four hoops against a C-class player, five against B-class, six against an A-class, but remember the top players are rather good at two-ball breaks (it is their most serious form of practice) and you may need the third ball more than they do.

As pegging out an opponent does not guarantee a win for you, when should you do it? If you are no further back than 1-back with your backward ball and your opponent's is for 4-back, think about it and go ahead; if he is for penult, think about it and decide against; if he is for rover, do not even think about it!

The Two-ball Ending

A game in which two balls have been pegged out, usually with one ball well ahead, can be even more exciting.

If you are behind, your tactics will depend on how far behind you are. A two-hoop disadvantage is not too serious, if you can get position at 4-back before your opponent can get position at rover. You will be able to get position at penult before he has made rover and he cannot trickle back to the peg. At worst, you will have a better shot at his ball than he has at the peg.

If you are further behind than two hoops, you will have to make up the deficit. If both balls have a long way to go and you feel you are the better touch player, you may be able to make up a couple of hoops, perhaps three, by playing follow-my-leader. Otherwise, you will have to hit in. Every time you do so should enable you to catch up one hoop, by dispersing your opponent's ball well away from its hoop while leaving yourself, with the continuation shot if necessary, in position for yours. Your best chance of hitting in may come when your opponent is going down the centre.

When you do hit in, a big roll to your next hoop in the hope of getting a two-ball break is not advisable: your chance of getting sufficient control from a long hoop approach is pretty slim; apart from that, you have nowhere to go if you fail to get reasonable position to run the hoop – you cannot take position because your opponent's ball is too close, and a wired position at your hoop will concede a lift. Instead, good players split to their next hoop with the opponent's ball going to the next hoop but one. It may mean a 14yd (12.8m) shot to hit in after you have run your hoop, but it offers the best chance to continue.

The tactics for the player in front are quite simple. Take position for your next hoop, unless to do so would leave your opponent a short- or medium-length shot. If you are a long way in front, it may pay to let your opponent have a hoop in order to get him out of the way. For example, let your opponent have 1-back before you approach penult.

Endings on Time

Most tournaments have a time-limit on each game. Fortunately the time-limit is fairly generous; at least three hours or three-and-a-quarter hours if double-banked. The games which run to time are usually between high-bisquers, who lack the skills to make breaks without the use of bisques. For other players there is little excuse, and a game which runs to time deserves to be put out of its misery.

When time is called, play continues for an extension period during which the striker completes his turn and his opponent has one more turn. The winner is the player who has scored the greater number of points.

If the scores are level at the end of the extension period, play continues and the winner is the player who scores the next point. In handicap games bisques may not be used during the extension period nor immediately after by the player in play.

As time approaches, use up your bisque allowance in handicap games (*see* Chapter 7). If you have a big lead, it is sensible to protect it by not taking risks but otherwise play your normal game at your normal pace. If you are in play when time is called, it is quite fair to disperse the balls at the end of your turn (the ideal position is a ball in each corner) to give your opponent little chance of making a break on his turn.

However, it is completely against the spirit in which the game is played to waste time or play entirely defensively, i.e. not try to make progress but merely stop your opponent from making progress, in order to win, and players who do so will get no encouragement from me.

7 Handicap Play

Bisques *(Figs 126 and 127)*

Croquet is fortunate in that there is a handicapping system which permits players of all abilities to play each other. Each player has a handicap set by the club handicapper or a CA handicapper. The handicap range is from –5 to 20 for CA tournament purposes, the lower handicap indicating the better player. Above 5 handicaps are adjusted in unit intervals, below 5 in half unit intervals. Above 12 the adjustment is usually in two-unit intervals, and may be extended for club play.

The weaker player receives the difference of the two handicaps in the form of bisques, each one allowing him to start a completely new turn immediately his previous one has finished. A half bisque, if taken, allows a restricted turn in which no point may be scored for any ball. The state of the handicap is indicated by an appropriate number of white-painted rods called bisques pushed into the ground at the side of the court. A bisque is removed by the opponent each time the player indicates that he wishes to take one.

This can lead to some difficulty for high-bisquers when they play each other, as neither player has sufficient bisques to make progress reasonably quickly. As an alternative, the laws permit full bisque play, where each player receives his full bisque allowance or a modified allowance.

The correct use of bisques is an important feature of handicap play. There are some players who proclaim that they do not know how to use bisques and that they play better when they have been used up. Well, more fool they! That is why their handicap is so high.

The Class System

Players are divided into classes according to their ability or handicap. The boundaries between the various classes are not fixed and may vary slightly from tournament to

Fig 126 George Chamberlin indicates that he wants to take a bisque.

Fig 127 Ted Scott acknowledges the bisque.

tournament according to the entry but, as a rough guide, are as follows:

A-class – Handicap below 2

These players, particularly the scratch and minus players, are quite capable of completing a game in two turns and will often create breaks from seemingly difficult positions. They are usually very good shots and would expect to hit at 10yd (9m) more often than they miss. These players should never be underestimated.

B-class – Handicap 2 to 5

These players are usually capable of taking a four-ball break round but may not be so proficient with the three-ball break, nor as capable of creating a break. Some may be very good shots but often they are not as consistent.

C-class – Handicap 5½ to 11

C-class players can play the four-ball break and will occasionally go right round in a single turn but usually break down somewhere along the way. A break of perhaps six hoops is more normal. They usually need bisques or an opponent breaking down to make the break, and their shooting is not so good.

D-class – Handicap 12 and over

These are usually players who have not been playing long and who do not make more than a few hoops in a turn. They often miss shortish roquets.

General Use of Bisques
(Figs 128 and 129)

Your bisques should be used to greatest effect to set up and maintain breaks, and you should always be looking for opportunities where the use of a single bisque will give you a break.

Consider, for example, the position in Fig 128. You have a simple rush on your partner ball to hoop 1 at the start of your turn and you can easily make hoop 1 off that ball, but what would you do next? After you have made hoop 1, there is no easy break for you even with the use of a bisque.

Instead, rush yellow to hoop 1 and take off to blue in the fourth corner. Roquet blue and play a split to put blue rather less than half-way between black and the peg, finishing with red close to black. Roquet black and play a straight drive to put black past the peg with a rush on blue towards the peg. Now play your continuation shot to give you a rush on blue to a spot where you can croquet it to hoop 2 as a pioneer. Take the bisque, rush and croquet blue as above, roquet black, take off to yellow and you have your four-ball break.

It may seem a bit complicated, but you have used all of the strokes permitted to you in order to make all of the shots easy ones. Note in particular that the pioneer for hoop 2 was placed from a relatively short distance. It would have been possible to put blue as the pioneer to hoop 2 directly from corner

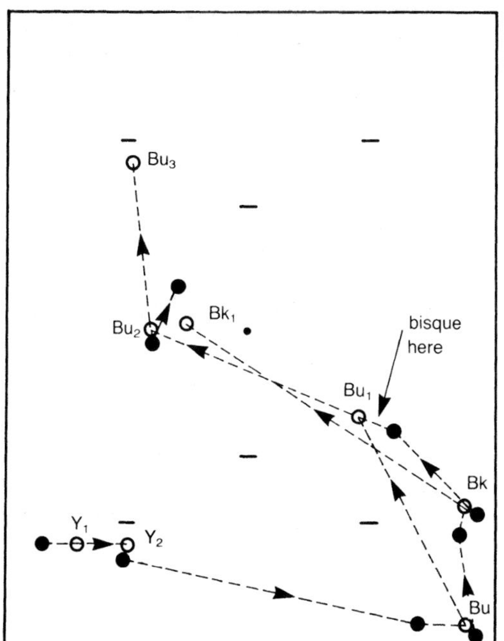

Fig 128 Constructing a four-ball break with a bisque.

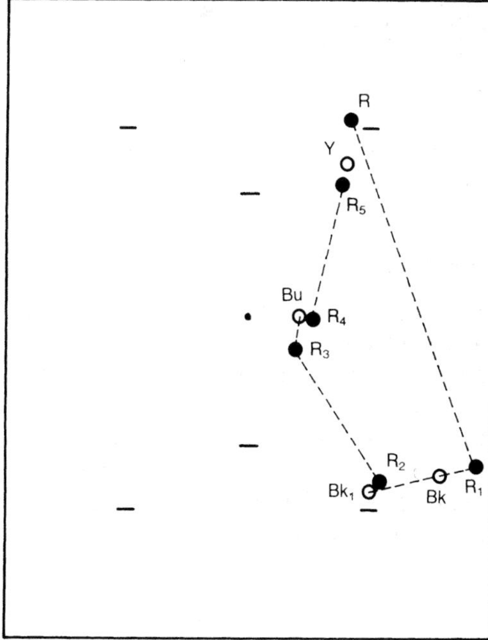

Fig 129 Tidying up a crumbling break with a bisque.

four, but it would not have been so easy from there. Remember to use all of the strokes to make the shots easy.

In general, if you have a rush to your hoop at the start of your turn, one bisque is all that is required to set up a four-ball break.

As you can see on pages 99–102 on openings against A-class players, it is usually possible to set up a four-ball break when you are the out-player with the use of two bisques but, if you are playing against opponents of lesser calibre, you should be looking for high profit situations for the use of your bisques. You get the maximum benefit from a bisque when you can use it to set up or rescue a four-ball break or prevent a stronger opponent having an easy four-ball break.

Look at Fig 129. Here your four-ball break has started to disintegrate. Your pioneer at hoop 3 was not very good and at hoop 4 it is even worse. You have failed to get position to run hoop 3 with a take-off from yellow. You could play your continuation shot to put red in front of the hoop, take a bisque and carry on from there, but you would have spent a bisque and still have a disintegrating break.

A better plan, and one which you should certainly adopt if black were a good pioneer at hoop 4, would be to play to the far side of yellow with the continuation shot, take a bisque and rush yellow to the playing side of hoop 3. However, in the situation described that does nothing for the poor pioneer at hoop 4.

Best of all is to play the continuation shot off the east boundary so that, when it is replaced, you can rush black into position at hoop 4 or into court where it can be placed with a croquet stroke. You have a fair margin of error and the shot you eventually choose will depend on the exact spot red goes off. You can then come back to yellow via blue and you have your four-ball break back under control. Note that you should come back via blue, even if you have rushed black into position; two short take-offs are better than one long one and, besides, blue is more or less on the required rush line for yellow.

Be prepared, therefore, to invest a bisque to tidy up a break and remember that a distant ball, particularly if it is just in court from a yard-line, will often be the ball to go to first.

Suppose you have a tidy four-ball break and you stick in a hoop. If you are making that hoop off your partner ball, you may be tempted to leave the position. After all, you say, I can make the hoop next turn and my partner ball is close at hand. But, in the meantime, your opponent will almost certainly have removed the pioneer from your next hoop and may even have hit in. Take the bisque and keep the four-ball break.

Above all, avoid bisque disasters. Do not try to run long, angled hoops on a break, in the hope that you may save a bisque. Fail and you may well find yourself with your ball in an 'unrunnable' position, needing to use two bisques to continue.

Be particularly careful to avoid the situation known as the 'windscreen wiper', where you miss a roquet from 3 or 4yd (2.7 or 3.6m) and find the return roquet is even longer and more 'missable'. If a ball is outside the range at which you are certain to hit, shoot gently, just hard enough to go no more than 2yd (1.8m) past, should you miss.

In general, you should use your bisques early in the game. Many players like to save a bisque or two to the end, in case they get into difficulties; but a bisque used at the start to set up a four-ball break from hoop 1 has far greater potential for scoring points than one saved until rover.

An exception to this rule is if you, as a high-bisquer, are receiving only one bisque from another high-bisquer or have reached the stage early in the game where you have only one bisque left. Save that bisque to set up a break from hoop 4: it is easier to make a break from hoop 4 to 1-back, because they are closer together and those extra points may be valuable in a timed ending.

Opening Against A-class Players *(Figs 130–5)*

You must not take any risks against these players. If you have five or more bisques, from the very beginning of the game you must try to win before your opponent has had the two turns that may be all he requires to win.

Suppose you win the toss. Put your opponent in: you need to take the first opportunity to play with all four balls on the court. Forget about the tice opening on pages 81–83 and play the following standard handicap opening.

After your opponent has played to the east boundary (red), play your first ball (blue) into court to the north-west of his ball as in Fig 130. The idea is eventually to croquet his ball to hoop 2 with your second ball (black), leaving that close to blue. Therefore, the exact spot you pick for your first ball will depend upon your drive ratio. Do you remember the practice exercise on page 37? Now you will appreciate its value.

As soon as you have played your first ball on to the court, your opponent will realise what you are up to. He may decide to play a waiting game and make things as difficult as possible for you, by playing yellow to the second corner.

Shoot with black at red on the east boundary and take a bisque (or, better, a half bisque, if you have one) if you miss. Now you can put the plan into action. Roquet red and

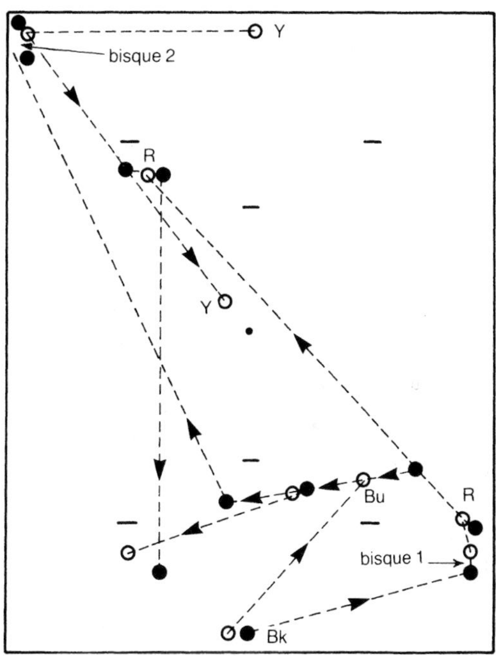

Fig 130 Standard opening against an A-class player.

croquet it to hoop 2 as described. If you are at the high end of the B class or low end of the C class, you might also try to get a rush on blue to hoop 1, but higher bisquers should concentrate on getting a good pioneer to hoop 2.

Roquet blue, rushing it in the direction of hoop 1 if possible, but do not try to make hoop 1 off blue unless you have rushed it within a yard or so of the hoop on the playing side. Instead, croquet blue as a good pioneer to hoop 1 and then shoot at yellow in the second corner. It does not matter if you hit or miss, because you will have to take another bisque before you can make hoop 1, but make certain you get close to yellow. Take your second bisque if you miss yellow, roquet it and croquet it to the peg with black finishing near red. Roquet red, take off to blue and away you go with the four-ball

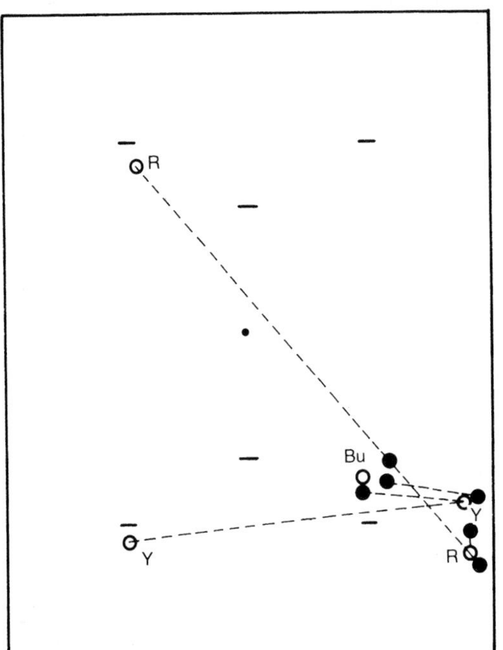

Fig 131 Standard opening after a missed third turn shot.

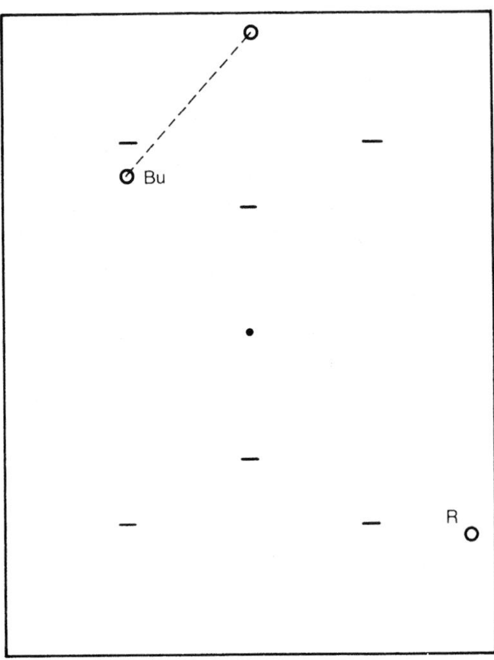

Fig 132 Alternative opening against an A-class player.

break at the cost of one and a half or two bisques.

However, your opponent may be in an attacking frame of mind and may decide to shoot at blue, hoping to get a three-ball break together, before you can get the fourth ball on the court. Suppose (or pray) that he misses, to leave the position of Fig 131.

Shoot at red, take a bisque or half bisque if necessary, and put it as a pioneer to hoop 2 as before. Roquet blue and take off back to yellow. Roquet yellow and croquet it as a pioneer to hoop 1. Play your continuation shot to leave a rush on blue to the peg if yellow is a good pioneer, or a rush more towards yellow if it is out of place. Take your second bisque to rush blue and you have your four-ball break.

A safer opening against an attacking A-class player is to put a pioneer in position at hoop 2 from the end of B baulk on the second turn. There is then little chance of him making a break on the third turn even if he hits either of the balls on court. Your continuation on the fourth turn is easier because you already have a pioneer at hoop 2. Shoot at whichever of his balls is closer to hoop 1 and use a bisque or half bisque if necessary to croquet it to hoop 1.

But, you may say, I only win the toss 50 per cent of the time on average. What do I do when I lose the toss? The answer is play safe. Play to the east boundary and shoot at your opponent's tice on the west boundary hard enough to finish in corner two if you miss. Your opponent will have a difficult job getting a break from this defensive position if he hits his tice, and may even leave the balls to your advantage if he fails to get going.

He will leave the position of Fig 133 if he misses. Then, shoot with red at blue, take a bisque or half bisque to roquet blue and play a stop shot to put it as a pioneer to hoop 1. Roquet black and put it as a pioneer to hoop 2. Shoot at yellow, take a bisque if you miss, and you have already transposed the position to that of the standard handicap opening. In fact, it is easier to get the break from the initial position of Fig 133, because the pioneers are put into position from closer range.

Once you have your break, keep it going with the use of bisques where necessary. If you reach 4-back with more than half of your bisques remaining, continue to the peg and set a defensive leave as in Fig 134. There is little your opponent can do even if he hits something. Never, in these circumstances, leave a ball anywhere near hoop 1 as in Fig 135. Faced with a losing position, any A-class player worth his salt will shoot with his other ball in order to pick up a break more easily. He would then go round himself and peg out your forward ball to devalue your remaining bisques. Of course, if he misses you have an easier position yourself, but the risk is not worth taking.

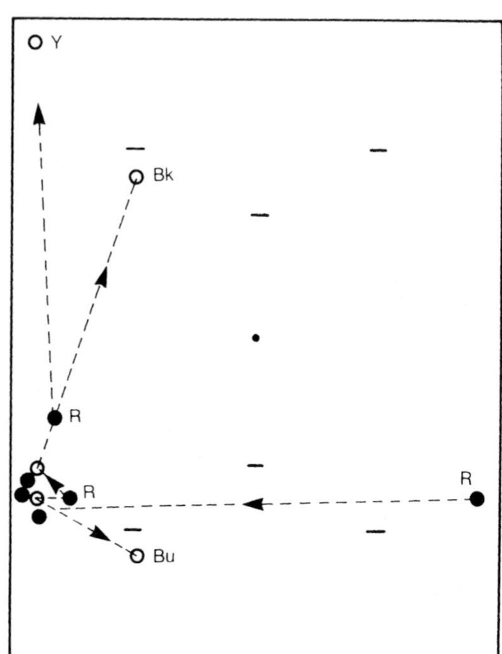

Fig 133 Setting up the four-ball break on the fifth turn.

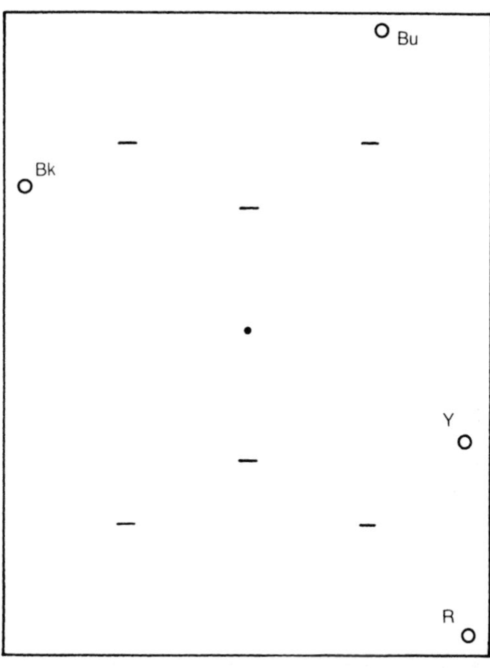

Fig 134 A good defensive leave for Ray.

If you reach 4-back with only half or just under half your bisques remaining, go to the peg with an attacking leave as in Fig 135. Now your opponent is less likely to gamble, because he has a chance if he plays safe. He will almost certainly remove the ball from hoop 1, but if he misses a shot, you should be able to set up your four-ball break with only one bisque.

If you have spent rather more than half of your bisques by the time you reach 4-back, you have little option but to gamble yourself.

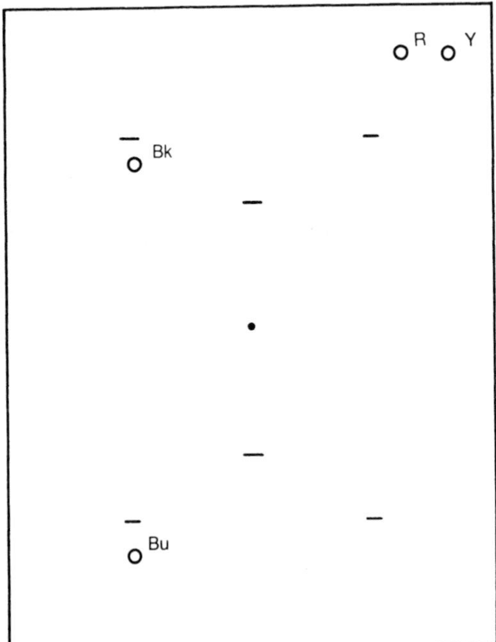

Fig 135 An attacking leave.

You need to set up your next break as economically as possible and win on your next turn. Go to the peg and leave an attacking leave as in Fig 135. It is your best chance of winning.

Tactics Against Other Than A-class Players

There is now less urgency to start quickly. Use the standard opening and look for the first opportunity to set up a break with one bisque. This will often occur if your opponent breaks down at hoop 1 or hoop 2. Then you will have a pioneer handy.

At the beginning of your turn consider whether you can use a bisque to set up a break. If you can with either ball, the break with the backward ball has greater potential.

Against a B-class player, take your forward ball as far as penult, unless your opponent has both balls past hoop 5; then you should go to rover. By stopping at penult there is little chance of being peeled and pegged out.

Against C-class players take one ball to rover, or even to peg if your opponent has both balls well back and you are close to home with your second ball.

Conceding Bisques

As your play improves, your handicap will come down and you will more often concede bisques to other players. Some players can make mincemeat of better players when they receive a few bisques, but struggle against weaker opposition when they have to concede them.

The tactics of conceding bisques are quite simple. Remember that your opponent will be looking for one-bisque opportunities, so do not give him any. This is going to impose some restriction on your normal game, but that is the penalty you pay for being the better player.

Be particularly careful at the start of the game. A speculative roll to hoop 1 will leave a pioneer for your opponent if it is unsuccessful. Instead, a speculative take-off may yield a hoop but, more importantly, will enable you to retreat to a safer position if it fails.

Once you have a break together, forget about your opponent and keep it going but, if you are still trying to get the break together, you should beware of putting a ball by one of your opponent's hoops, unless you are confident of making your next hoop.

High-bisquers

Under the normal handicap system, where the weaker player receives the difference in the two handicaps, two high-bisquers often struggle because they lack the skills to play breaks without needing the occasional bisque. One has only a few bisques, the other none at all.

It makes a good deal of sense for high-bisquers to play full bisque games: that is, each player receives his normal handicap as bisques. Both players then have the benefit of practice in playing breaks as well as learning of the dangers when conceding bisques. A better alternative is to play with each player receiving six or eight bisques less than his handicap. It is then highly unlikely that either player will be able to finish in two turns, and each will have to look for high profit situations. This makes the game more competitively interactive than the full bisque game.

8 Advanced Play

Optional Lift or Contact

(Figs 136 and 137)

As described on pages 88–90, expert players became adept at taking the first break to the peg, leaving the opponent's balls cross-wired at hoop 1 and laying up with a rush from corner three. The opponent had a shot of some 30 to 35yd (27 to 31.5m) with the prospect of a lost game if he missed. It was clearly necessary to change the laws to make the game less one-sided. Over the years various additions, which apply specifically to advanced play, have been made to the laws.

The present position is that the opponent is entitled to an optional lift if the striker's ball has scored 1-back or 4-back for itself in the preceding turn. In addition, if the striker's ball has scored both 1-back and 4-back

Fig 136 David Maugham.

Fig 137 Martin Murray.

in the same turn and its partner ball had not scored 1-back before that turn, the opponent is entitled to an optional contact. However, if a player has pegged out any ball, he is not entitled to these options.

If the opponent takes a lift, he may play either of his balls from any point on either baulk-line. If he takes the contact, he may place either of his balls in contact with any other ball and take croquet immediately.

The disadvantange of losing the innings by conceding contact is so great that few players take the first ball beyond 3-back in a break. The optional lift usually reduces the length of the opponent's shot and makes it easier for him to hit in.

Games between expert players are less one-sided and tactical variety has increased with the leaves that have evolved. As a further advantage, the triple peel, where the partner ball is peeled through its last three hoops and both balls are pegged out, has added interest to the game.

Lift Leaves

For the purposes of discussion of the following lift leaves we assume that Ray is in play with red; blue and black are interchangeable.

The Old Standard Leave (OSL) (Fig 138)

The OSL is shown in Fig 138. Blue is usually positioned after 1-back; 2-back and 3-back are made with a three-ball break. Yellow can be rushed to the boundary either from the peg or from 3-back. This is the commonest leave in advanced play, because it is very easy to arrange. A missed lift shot or a defensive play give good opportunities for a break. The main and crucial disadvantage

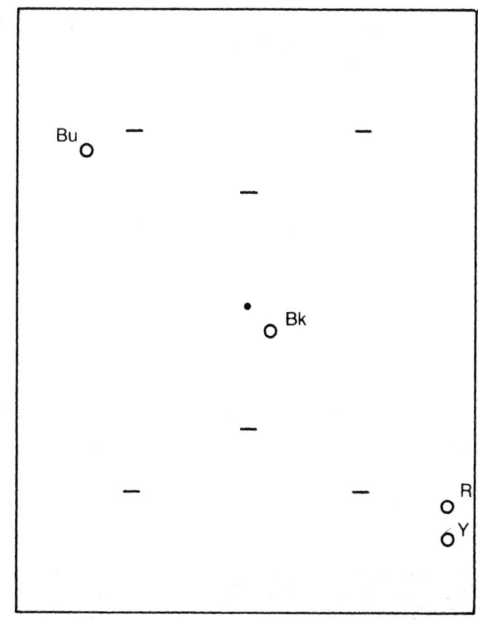

Fig 138 The old standard leave.

is that the so-called short lift shot from the end of A baulk is only some 14yd (12.8m). A top-class shot will have at least a 50 per cent chance of hitting, with equal opportunity to make a break.

However, if the lift is missed, there is an excellent opportunity to pick up a break with a good possibility of a triple attempt. The continuation for Ray is to stop shot the opponent's ball towards hoop 4, leaving a rush on the partner ball to blue or black. The partner ball is then croqueted to hoop 2, leaving a rush on blue or black to hoop 1. To attempt to make hoop 1 directly off red would leave Bab with another short shot if the attempt were unsuccessful.

The New Standard Leave (NSL) (Fig 139)

The NSL is shown in Fig 139. As with the OSL, blue is positioned after 1-back. 2-back

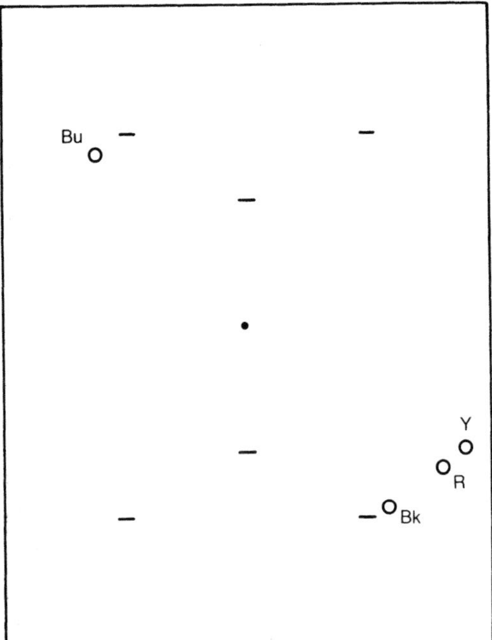

Fig 139 The new standard leave.

is made off its pioneer, which is then rushed towards 3-back. Both yellow and black are played to the north-east of 3-back, so that black can be roqueted and croqueted slightly to the north-east of hoop 4. Yellow is then taken to the east boundary, hidden from the end of A baulk by hoop 4, and red is left in position to be rushed towards hoop 4.

Bab is hampered from taking the very short shot with black at red or yellow by hoop 4. The lift from A or B baulks is much longer than that for the OSL. The usual lift is for Bab to shoot from B baulk with blue, finishing in or near fourth corner if it misses.

The continuation for Ray with yellow after the missed lift is to roquet red gently, go to blue and croquet it to hoop 2, leaving a rush on black to hoop 1. The croquet shot from the fourth corner is a big shot and needs practice.

If Bab plays blue defensively into the third corner, it is much more difficult for Ray to get a break but the opportunity for Bab to hit in has been lost.

The Diagonal Spread (Fig 140)

The diagonal spread has the advantage of the NSL of leaving a long lift shot plus the advantage of the OSL of good possibilities of a break from a missed lift. Blue is cross-pegged from black and Bab is hampered by the peg from shooting at red and yellow with black.

To arrange this leave, position the partner ball and one opposition ball close to the peg before making 3-back off the other opposition ball. The 3-back pilot is croqueted towards the west boundary and the position of the opposition ball is adjusted by the peg, using the partner ball as an escape ball.

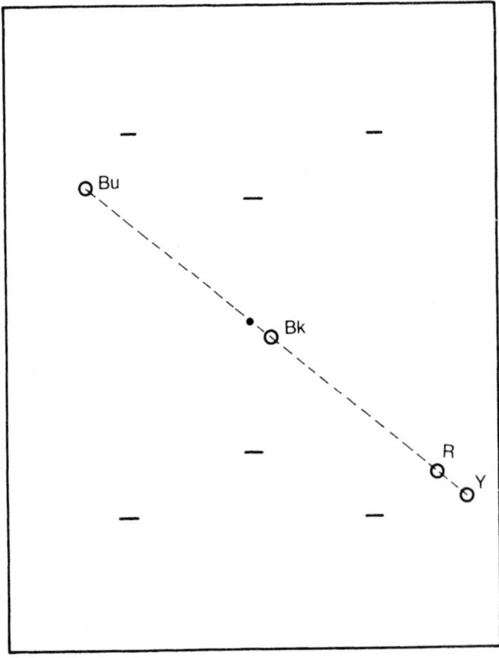

Fig 140 The diagonal spread.

Whichever ball is lifted, Ray has a rush on red to the other ball after a missed lift.

The Vertical Spread (*Fig 141*)

This leave is most useful when Ray has taken yellow to the peg with possibly one peel on red on the way, to finish with the clips on peg and penult. Blue and black are positioned at penult and rover with the aid of an escape ball as for a peel. Yellow, of course, is the escape ball at rover but the escape ball at penult can be either black or yellow.

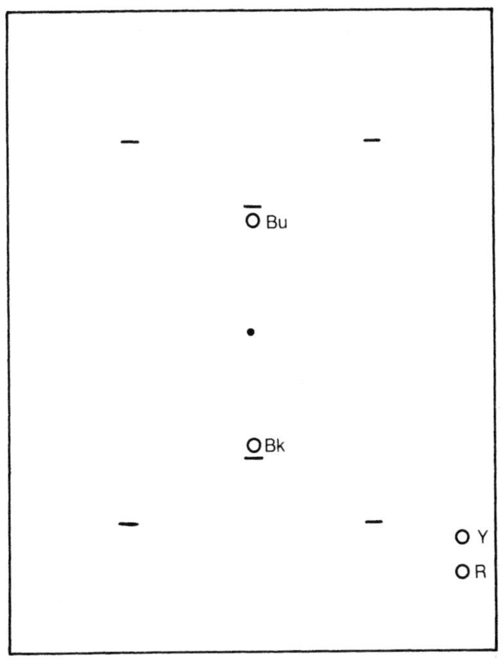

Fig 141 The vertical spread.

Choice of Lift Shot

When your opponent has taken a ball round to 4-back, you will be faced with the lift shot. Remember that the lift (or contact) is optional and you may play a ball as it lies. However, in most cases your opponent will have finished with a reasonable leave. Your choice should be conditioned by your own shooting ability and your opponent's ability as a player.

If you can genuinely hit the 14yd (12.8m), or so-called short, lift shot more than 50 per cent of the time, it will pay on average to take this shot. Even if you are not such a good shot, you should still take the shortest shot available to you if you are playing a strong opponent, i.e. one who is likely to go round with his second ball whichever shot you miss.

Against a weaker opponent it may be better to take a longer shot but one which leaves a safer position if missed.

The Triple Peel

The triple peel or TP is the goal of most players in advanced play. However, only a few top players have the skill and control to complete a TP regularly; other A-class players (and some B-class players) try but succeed only occasionally.

The mechanics of the standard triple peel are quite simple. The 4-back peel is made immediately after the striker's ball has run hoop 3, leaving a rush on the escape ball to the east of the pioneer at hoop 4. The penult peel is made immediately after the striker's ball has run hoop 6, leaving a rush on the escape ball to the north boundary to the side of 1-back. The rover peel is made either on the croquet stroke sending the striker's ball to the pioneer at 2-back or 3-back or as a straight peel at rover.

A more detailed discussion of the triple peel is beyond the scope of this book. The reader is referred instead to *The World of Croquet* by John McCullough and Stephen Mulliner (The Crowood Press) or *Expert Croquet Tactics* by Keith Wylie.

If you play for fun, an attempt at a TP is great fun. If you play to win, your safest course is to forget about the TP and to take the second ball to the peg with the easiest possible break and finish with a good leave.

You need to be able to play accurate croquet strokes, run hoops with control and rush the ball well to become a regular triple peeler. I recommend the three-ball break as the best practice. If you can take a controlled three-ball break round twenty-four hoops, i.e. returning to hoop 1 after running rover, then try a practice triple for fun. If you cannot, keep practising. In the long run it will be worth while; you will become a good player more quickly than if you are endlessly practising triple peels.

9 Tournament Play

CA TOURNAMENTS

Members of the CA (except non-tournament members) receive every February a fixture list of the coming season's tournaments. The tournaments are divided into championships, invitation events, week tournaments, open weekend tournaments and handicap weekend tournaments.

Championships and invitation events are restricted by handicap or grading to the best players. A week tournament usually lasts from Monday to Saturday and contains a number of events. As well as a handicap event open to all and possibly a handicap doubles event with weak and strong payers paired together, the players are divided into classes to compete on level terms within the classes. To maximise the number of games played at weekend tournaments, the format is usually Egyptian, where available players with similar numbers of wins are matched. The winner is the player with the highest percentage of wins.

When croquet was played mainly by the well-to-do and leisured, week tournaments were the only form open to all but now weekend tournaments have taken over as the most popular form. Each tournament has a manager, a tournament referee assisted by assistant referees, and a handicapper.

The fixture list contains details of all of these tournaments, plus copies of a standard entry form. Some tournaments fill up very quickly, so early application is advisable.

The manager, who normally also plays in the tournament, has a difficult task in keeping the tournament to schedule, especially at weekend tournaments, which are normally arranged to give everyone as many games as possible. You can help him by arriving on time and reporting your presence, and remember that you should be changed and ready to play by the official starting time. Competitors who arrive late with the exclamation 'What a terrible place to find!' are not appreciated. Read the tournament notices to see if there are any changes to the conditions applying to the tournament.

At the conclusion of the game the winner should report the result promptly to the manager but, if he is in the middle of a break in his game, do let him finish it first.

If it is your first tournament, let the tournament secretary know when you apply; then the manager can be informed. A good manager will pair you off with a more experienced player, usually a low-handicap player for whom the result is not too important, who will be able to advise you when necessary. Everybody is nervous at their first tournament, but there is really no need to be; croquet is a very friendly game.

Play

At the start of the game the player with the lower handicap usually spins the coin and he is responsible for setting out the correct number of bisques in a handicap game.

There is a law which enjoins players to play reasonably quickly but this does not mean that you are not allowed to play with normal care. A lot of time can be saved by paying attention when you are the outplayer, so that you know what you want to do as soon as your turn starts, and by walking quickly between shots when you are the in-player. After a long take-off, for example, walk after the ball as soon as you have completed your follow-through, rather than stand waiting until the ball has stopped rolling.

When you run a hoop in order, remove the clip and keep it until the end of your turn, then replace it on its correct hoop. If you roquet a ball off the court, you should replace it (with your back towards the court) before picking up your own ball, unless you are absolutely certain that you will be able to replace it exactly by reference to some feature off the court.

During the game you and your opponent act as joint referees and you should declare your own faults (for example, failing to shake or move a croqueted ball) even if your opponent is not watching. Pay attention to the game even when you are the out-player. Although in friendly play players often stop their opponents from committing an error, it is expressly forbidden by the laws.

If you see that your opponent has committed an error, for example, playing with the wrong ball or running the wrong hoop, you should forestall his play immediately. You may lose your right to redress the error if you wait too long and exceed the limit of claims. If you cannot agree with your opponent, you are not entitled to seek an outsider's opinion without your opponent's permission but you may ask for a referee.

You are entitled to ask your opponent anything concerning the state of the game. The out-player should point out immediately if clips or balls are misplaced.

Calling a Referee

At some time during the course of the game you may need to call for a referee. All you have to do is raise your mallet, head uppermost, and look around expectantly. You should call for a referee whenever you feel that you may commit a fault on any stroke; the most common cases are when there is a possibility of playing a crush shot or when you have a hampered swing. In general, beginners tend to call for a referee when one is not really required, but it is better that way round than the other.

When the referee arrives, do not assume that he will know immediately why he has been called; explain the position to him and give him time to mark the positions of any balls. He will then probably ask you to take up your stance but do not strike the ball until he tells you. He will need some time to find the best position to watch the shot.

If the referee declares a fault, he will probably explain why. You are entitled to ask if he does not, but do so politely. You are entitled to appeal to the tournament referee against a referee's decision on a matter of law but not on a matter of fact.

Double-banking

In order to give everyone as many games as possible at most tournaments two games take place simultaneously. In the second game pink and white, and brown and green balls are used in place of red and yellow, and black and blue. This is known as double-banking.

There is almost inevitably some interference between the two games but, with care, it can be kept to a minimum. Each player should carry small coins to act as markers for balls which have to be removed temporarily to allow the other game to progress. If a ball from the other game is in your way, you should ask the in-player in that game for permission to mark it, if it is not in a critical position. However, time your request carefully; nobody likes to be interrupted if he is about to try a difficult hoop.

Precedence should be given to the game in which a player is making a break or, if neither player is making a break and they are approaching the same hoop, to the player who makes the first roquet towards the hoop. If both players are making a break and approaching the same hoop, precedence is given to the player who is more likely to get clear of the hoop first.

You should always be aware of the other game and take care not to walk across the line of aim of another player, especially when stepping on to the court.

If you sit with the out-player from the other game, remember that he will probably be concentrating on his own game; he will not appreciate a post-mortem on your last turn when you resume your seat.

The End of the Game

A friendly wave of thanks from the centre of the court from the winner and a similar acknowledgement from the loser is all that is required at the end of the game, although some players like to shake hands. The winner should remove the balls from the court and place them in the ball-box with the clips.

Most winners offer to buy their opponent a drink, but this is by no means obligatory. Remember that not all players who win regularly, particularly if they are juniors or retired, have the means to do so.

You may wish to discuss the game with your opponent but do not stand around on the court to do so, particularly if a double-banked game is still in progress; your first duty is to report the result to the manager and to find out when you are likely to be required to play again. After that you can discuss the game to your heart's content with your opponent, but do not assume that everyone around will want a detailed description of your fortune or misfortune.

10 Winning Croquet

How Much Do You Want to Win?

This may seem a strange question to ask, for croquet is a competitive game, after all, and the object of the game is to get both balls round and peg out before your opponent, but croquet has other facets which many players enjoy more. It is an intricate and beautiful game which offers something extra to players of all abilities.

At one level, the first all-round break without the use of bisques is memorable, but may lead to risky play on the way. At another level, many B-class players try desperately for their first, elusive, triple peel and sacrifice dozens of games in the attempt.

The urge to attempt some play that you have not managed before can be very strong, but this is not the best way to win. Winning players are usually consistent players and they achieve this consistency by knowing their ability and playing within it. However, there is also the balance between long-term and short-term aims to be taken into account. If you never try to extend your ability in competitive play, you will eventually reach the stage where you stop improving.

If the competitive drive in you is very strong, you will want to win frequently; if you are more interested in the way you play, then winning will be a bonus which you accept gratefully. It is pointless to argue whether the better player is the one who wins more often or the one who is capable on occasion of more skilful play. The choice is yours, as is the way you play. Perhaps the best compromise would be to treat friendly games as opportunities to experiment and play more carefully in tournaments.

Playing the Odds

Even those who are less dedicated to winning will play in tournaments in which they are keen to do well. In general, as I have already indicated, it pays to play within your ability. If you must make a speculative approach to a hoop off your partner ball, make sure that you play it near a boundary where you can retreat with a good leave if the approach is not successful. Consider whether a good leave might not be a better plan altogether. In other words, play safe when you have the innings.

An exception to this general rule is in level play when your opponent is a far stronger player. Then it is too much to hope that he will descend to your level; you must try to raise your game and be prepared to take more risks. 'Win quickly' is a good maxim, for the longer the game goes on, the more likely your opponent's superior skill will prevail.

When you are the out-player, your choice will lie between shooting or playing safe. This is the time when you have to assess the odds. You should have a reasonable idea of the probability of hitting the shot depending upon the distance. Fig 142 shows the probability of hitting as a function of distance for various types of player. The different curves

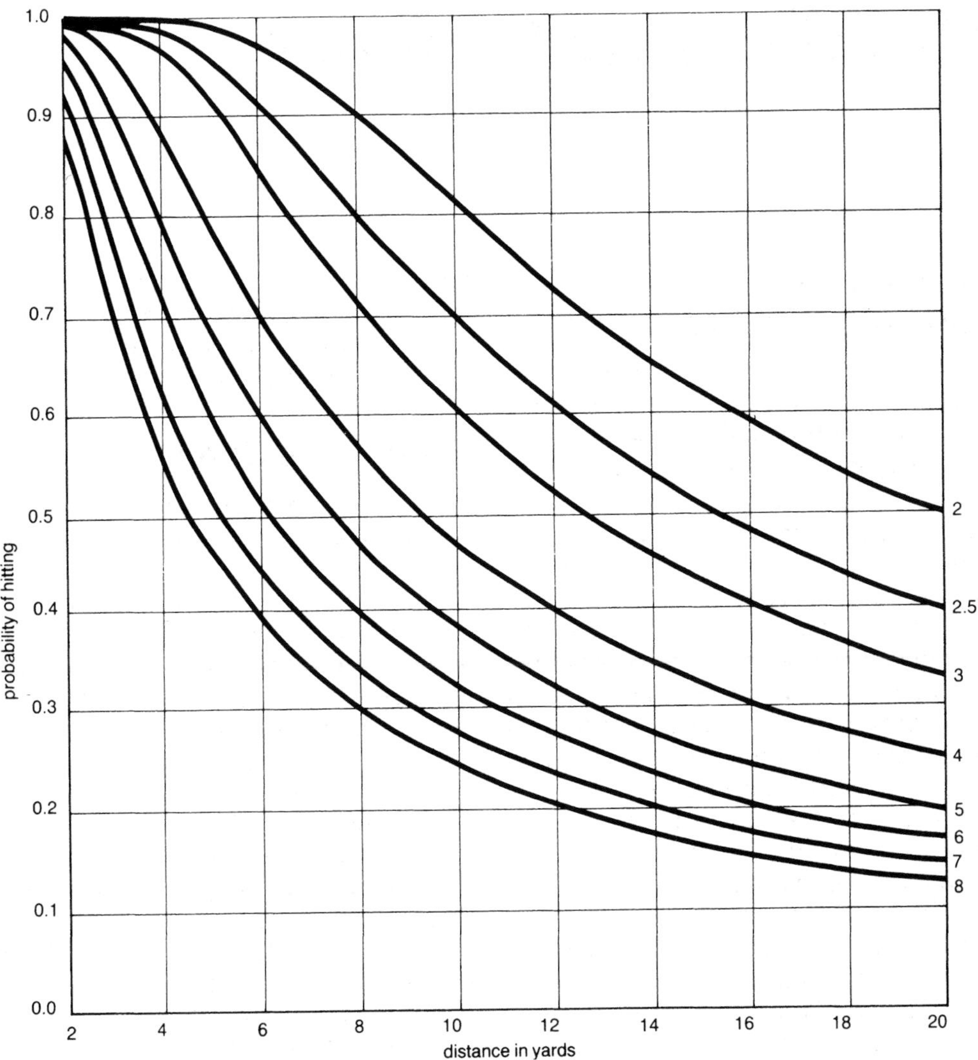

Fig 142 Probability of hitting a single ball target as a function of distance. The RH scale is the inverse proportion of times a player would hit the peg from 14 yards.

represent the frequency with which a player of that type would hit the centre peg when shooting from a side boundary. The average for C- and D-class players would probably be between one hit in six and one hit in eight. A good shot is defined as someone who would hit the peg with one shot in four. The very best shots might achieve one hit in two.

Try this exercise. Shoot from the full 14yd (12.8m) and remember to treat each shot with the same care that you would normally. You will need to take at least twenty-four shots to avoid spurious results. When you have found which curve represents your ability, you will be able to determine your probability of hitting at other distances. You will have to bear in mind that your ability may vary by about one curve each way, depend-

Fig 143 Stephen Mulliner.

ing on whether at the time you feel you are shooting well, averagely or badly.

That is not all, however: you must also take into account the ratio of reward to risk. What do you gain, apart from the innings (and that is important), if you hit, compared with what your opponent gains, if you miss? The product of the hit/miss probability ratio and the reward/risk ratio is the true assessment of whether to shoot or not. If the product is greater than one, shoot.

An example of a very high reward/risk ratio is the free shot at your opponent's joined-up balls by your hoop. Miss and you will end up safely on a boundary; hit and you will gain a three-ball break. The ratio is so high that you should shoot even if the probability of hitting is low. On the other hand, suppose that your opponent is guarding the boundary. Now the reward/risk ratio is less than 1 (if you hit the ball by the hoop, you will probably knock it away from its position as a good pioneer); the hit/miss probability should be much greater than 1 for the shot to be worth while. Your opponent's ability should also be taken into account when assessing the reward/risk ratio.

These are clear-cut examples; other cases are less so. I am not suggesting that you have to do these mental calculations every time you are faced with a shot. It would be impossible, in any case, to put exact figures into them, but you should be aware of the implications of every shot that you take and the probable outcome. Try the exercise, though, and you will gradually acquire a feel for the right tactics.

If you do decide not to take a shot, you will have to play safe. As a general consideration, you should move the ball which is most useful to your opponent, i.e. a pioneer ball at his next hoop or next hoop but one or a ball in the middle of the court. Remember also to take your opponent's ability into account. If you decide to join up with your partner ball, the width of the join could be as little as 1yd (91cm) against a C-class player, but should not be less than 8yd (7.2m) against an A-class player. Alternatively, you may decide to put the ball in a corner; if so, choose a corner behind the opponent's break. Against an A-class player, play the ball not into the corner but off the court so that it will be replaced on the yard-line about 1ft (30cm) away from the corner to avoid the risk of a corner cannon.

Mental Preparation

You will be faced from time to time with a critical shot, often at the distance you like least. You feel you should hit, but you often miss. In the jargon of the garrulous sports commentator, you are feeling the pressure.

Ask yourself for a moment where this pressure comes from. It is entirely self-imposed. You want to win: fair enough, but do you want to win too much? The more importance you place upon winning, the greater the pressure is likely to be and the more likely you are to miss! This is an example of your conscious mind getting in the way of the subconscious. All the practice you have put in to groove your swing is being nullified by outside thoughts. Convince yourself that winning is hardly likely to change your life drastically, and you will be well on the way to avoiding pressure. After all, a 10yd (9m) roquet is a 10yd roquet, whether it is in practice or the final of a competition.

In a similar way, fear of failure, particularly against a weaker opponent, can be just as destructive as wanting to win too much. The fear of missing the shot makes it more probable that you will do so. Again, try to get things back into proportion. Missing a roquet comes pretty low on the scale of human disasters!

You should never approach a critical shot with either of these two thoughts in your mind. If it happens to you, step away; think of something else and relax. Be confident and you will be more successful. The exercise on page 23 on roquets was designed to build up your confidence as well as groove your swing.

Now, I realise that this is the counsel of perfection; avoid pressure and you will not have to cope with it. If you do feel pressure, you have to do something about it. The physiological effect is one of tension; increased heart rate, perhaps even muscle tremor. The opposite of stress is relaxation and relaxation techniques can be a great help. Deep-breathing exercises in which you become aware of your breathing or your heartbeat will help you to relax. So will allowing your mind to drift to soothing thoughts; waves lapping against the shore or slow, soft music, for example.

Fig 144 Debbie Cornelius.

This all takes time, unless you are particularly skilled at instant relaxation, so give yourself time. You also need to have or to create your own space in order to do this. If you have been chatting to spectators, walk away. Start your relaxation well before your opponent's turn has come to an end and you will be prepared. Play the shot through in your mind and picture the successful outcome in as much detail as you can, in order to distract your conscious mind from worry. Let your subconscious mind take over and it will take care of your swing.

Confidence is very important. You should reinforce your confidence as much as possible. Every good player has purple patches when everything goes well: it seems that you cannot miss a long roquet, your croquet strokes are played to within inches, hoops are run with perfect control. It is like playing on a different plane, floating through the game as if in a dream. What has happened is that you have let your subconscious mind take over the playing of shots, once your conscious mind has decided which shot to play. The two are working in perfect harmony. There is no need to calculate how hard to hit or how much roll is required – the feel is there in your hands and your body. You have been completely relaxed about it all.

When it happens, enjoy the experience and remember it. After the game go away quietly and replay in your mind every single shot. Do the same in the evening and the next day, and the game will be fixed in your memory to draw on when you need to. Give your confidence a boost when you need to by deliberately remembering these games and how well you can play. By the same token, forget the disasters immediately; you do not need them so wipe them out of your mind.

PREPARATION FOR TOURNAMENTS

Circumstances do not always permit sensible preparation for a tournament that is important to you, but you should try to prepare. You cannot get up early in the morning, drive two hundred miles to get there for a 9.30 a.m. start and expect realistically to be playing at your best. Even if you succeed, tiredness will probably catch up with you in another game later in the day. Travel the day or evening before and get a good night's sleep.

In many sports players cannot retain peak form throughout a season. They train to bring themselves to a peak for the events that matter, with a period of relaxation followed by a period of intensive practice. Many of our top players play relatively infrequently. Take a leaf out of their book by not playing any competitive croquet in the week or fortnight before the tournament. Use your time to work on the weaknesses in your game. Arive at the tournament hungry to play.

Learning to Improve

Many players reach a plateau in their performance which is below their potential. In many cases this is because their game has got into a rut, either tactically or technically, and they have not realised it. They go on playing the game in the same way, using the same strokes and the same tactics which have stood them in good stead on their way down through the handicap range. They do not appreciate that becoming a better player is not just a matter of sticking in fewer hoops or missing fewer roquets. Good players have a command of all the strokes but make the game easier for themselves by thoughtful play.

If you have reached a plateau or want to improve more quickly, do not be afraid to ask a better player for advice after a game, whether you have won or lost. Most players are pleased to be asked, although not many will offer unsolicited advice, perhaps because advice is not always welcome. Listen to the comments of knowledgeable players when they are watching others in play and ask yourself whether they would apply to your play. Perhaps a CA coaching course could help you to rethink your game.

Think, practise and you can become the club champion or, who knows, world champion. But, whatever your ambition, you will have a lot of fun on the way!

Glossary

Address Placing the mallet head behind the striker's ball before playing a stroke.

Advanced play A variation which entitles the opponent to a lift if the striker has run 1-back or 4-back, or a contact if both have been run in a single turn before the partner ball has scored 1-back.

All-round break A 12 hoop break.

Angle of swing The angle between the line of centres of the balls and the line of swing of the mallet in a croquet stroke.

Back spin Where the top of the ball is rotating in the opposite direction to that of travel.

Back swing The backward movement of the mallet.

Backward ball The ball which has most hoops to make.

Backward take-off A take-off hoop approach from the non-playing side.

Ball in hand A ball which has made or is deemed to have made a roquet.

Baulk The start line on either the south boundary (A baulk) or the north boundary (B baulk).

Big split A split croquet stroke where both balls are sent a long distance.

Bisque A coloured rod placed in the ground to indicate in handicap play that a player is entitled to an extra turn.

Break A turn in which the striker's ball runs more than one hoop.

Break down To make a mistake which brings the turn to an end.

Cannon A croquet stroke in which the roqueted ball is in contact with a third or fourth ball.

Centre style Style of play where the mallet is swung between the legs.

Chop roll A roll stroke where the inclined mallet is driven on to the ball to induce forward spin.

Class system The division of players according to their handicaps.

Clips Coloured markers to indicate the next hoop for each ball.

Contact Placing the striker's ball next to another ball to play a croquet stroke.

Continuation stroke The extra stroke played after running a hoop or playing a lawful croquet stroke.

Control The play of a ball to a required position.

Corner-ball A ball on a corner spot.

Corner cannon A cannon from the immediate vicinity of a corner.

Corner spot The intersection of two yard-lines.

Croquet stroke A stroke where, after the striker's ball has been placed in contact with a roqueted ball, both balls are moved.

Croqueted ball A ball which is moved by the striker's ball in a croquet stroke.

Cross-peg To arrange the opponent's balls so that neither can hit the other because the peg is between them.

Cross-wire To arrange the opponent's balls so that neither can hit the other because a hoop is between them.

Crush A fault where the striker's ball is squeezed by the mallet against a hoop or the peg.

Cut rush A rush played at an angle to the line of swing.

Diagonal spread A particular leave in advanced play.

Distance ratio The relative distances moved by the croqueted ball and the striker's ball in a croquet stroke.

Dolly rush A simple rush where the two balls are close together.

Double Two balls which subtend a target angle twice that of a single ball.

Double-banking Playing two simultaneous games on a single court.

Double peel A turn in which the partner ball is peeled through penult and rover and pegged out.

Double tap A fault where the striker's ball is struck more than once.

Drag The action of a mallet on the striker's ball in a croquet stroke which draws the ball in towards the line of swing.

Drive The normal action of a croquet stroke.

Glossary

Escape ball A ball which may be croqueted easily after a peel.
Fault An illegal stroke incurring a penalty.
Follow-through The continuation of the swing after the ball has been struck.
Forward ball The ball that has the fewest hoops to make.
Forward spin Spin where the top of the ball is rotating in the direction of travel.
Forward swing The movement of the mallet in the forward direction prior to impact.
Four-ball break A break using all four balls.
Four-ball cannon A cannon resulting from a four-ball group.
Four-ball group Four balls in contact, one of which is a yard-line ball.
Full-bisque game A form of handicap play where each player may receive a bisque allowance.
Full roll A croquet stroke where the croqueted ball travels the same distance as the striker's ball.
Furniture A colloquial term for the hoops and the peg.
Getaway ball *see* escape ball.
Guarding a boundary Playing to the boundary close to the line of the opponent's open shot at your partner ball.
Half bisque A bisque entitling a player to an extra turn with the restriction that no point may be scored for any ball.
Half jump A jump shot which moves the ball being jumped.
Half roll A roll stroke where the striker's ball travels half the distance of the croqueted ball.
Hammer shot A stroke played downwards on to the ball with one's back to the target ball.
Hampered shot A shot where the normal swing of the mallet is impeded by a hoop, the peg or another ball.
Handicap A number which indicates someone's standard of play for handicap events.
Handicap play A form of play intended to give players of different abilities an equal chance.
High-bisquer A high-handicap player.
Hit-in To gain the innings by making a roquet.
Hoop approach A croquet stroke played to put the striker's ball in front of its next hoop.
Innings A player has the innings if he is in play.
In-player The player who has the innings.
Irish grip A grip with both palms facing forwards.
Irish peel A croquet stroke where both balls are sent through a hoop.
Jaws The area between the uprights of a hoop.
Join up To play the striker's ball at the end of a turn close to its partner ball.
Jump shot A stroke played downwards on to a ball to cause it to leave the ground.
Lay up To leave one's balls in a favourable position.
Leave The arrangement of balls at the end of a turn.
Level play A form of play without handicaps.
Lift The right to pick up a ball and play it from either baulk.
Line of centres The line joining the centres of two balls placed for a croquet stroke.
Low-bisquer A low-handicap player.
Middle-bisquer A player with an intermediate handicap.
Minus player A player with a handicap below zero.
New standard leave (NSL) A particular leave in advanced play.
Non-playing side The far side of the hoop with respect to the direction in which it is run.
Old standard leave (OSL) A particular leave in advanced play.
Open shot A shot where the target ball is not hidden by furniture.
Opening The play of the balls on to the court.
Out-player The player who does not have the innings.
Pass roll A roll stroke where the striker's ball travels further than the croqueted ball.
Peel The play of a ball through its next hoop by another ball.
Peelee A ball that is intended to be peeled.
Peg out To score a peg point with a ball and remove it from the game.
Penultimate (Penult) The last hoop but one.
Pilot The ball which is intended to be roqueted after running a hoop.
Pioneer An opponent's ball or the partner ball placed in position by a hoop yet to be run by the striker's ball.
Pivot A ball near the centre of the court in a four-ball break.

Playing side The side from which the hoop is to be run.
Position The spot to which a single ball is played (usually to run a hoop).
Pull a) The effect on a croqueted ball causing it to move in a line away from the line of centres towards the line of swing. b) A fault in a hammer stroke where the mallet maintains contact with the striker's ball for an appreciable period or accelerates the ball after the initial contact.
Push A fault in a normal stroke where contact is maintained between the mallet and ball for an appreciable period or the ball is accelerated after the initial contact.
Roll A croquet stroke where the distance ratio is less than that of a drive.
Roquet To hit another ball with the striker's ball.
Rover a) The last hoop. b) A ball which has scored the last hoop.
Run a hoop To hit a ball through its next hoop to score a point.
Rush To roquet a ball to a required position.
Rush line The direction of the rush.
Rush peel A peel achieved with a rush.
Scatter shot An attempt to manoeuvre another ball to a less disastrous position with the last stroke of the turn.
Scratch player A player with a zero handicap.
Second colours Green, pink, brown and white balls used for the second game in double-banking.
Shepherding A fault in a croquet stroke where the striker's ball is guided by the mallet after the croqueted ball has departed.
Shoot To attempt to roquet a ball when one is the out-player.
Short lift The lift shot taken at the opponent's balls after the OSL in advanced play.
Side style The style of play where the mallet is swung to the side of the body.
Single-ball stroke A stroke which causes only the striker's ball to move.
Single peel A break in which a ball is peeled through rover and pegged out.
Solomon grip A grip with the knuckles of both hands facing forwards.
Split A croquet stroke where the croqueted ball and the striker's ball travel in different directions.
Squeeze A leave which yields a potential break whichever ball the opponent moves.
Stalk To line up a shot by walking towards the striker's ball in the direction of the line joining it and the target ball.
Stance The position of the feet and body when playing a stroke.
Standard grip A grip with the knuckles of the upper hand facing forwards and of the lower hand facing backwards.
Standard triple A triple peel where the first two peels are achieved immediately after the striker's ball has run the hoop in the opposite direction.
Stop shot A croquet stroke where the distance ratio is greater than that of a drive.
Straight shot A croquet stroke where the croqueted ball and the striker's ball travel in the same direction.
Straight peel A peel which is achieved in the stroke before the striker's ball runs the same hoop.
Straight triple A triple peel where all the peels are straight peels.
Striker The in-player or the player about to play.
Striker's ball The ball which the striker has chosen to play.
Take a bisque To start a new turn in handicap play immediately after your previous turn has finished.
Take-off A croquet stroke played with a swing angle greater than 45 degrees.
Take position A single ball stroke played to put the ball in a required position (usually in front of a hoop).
Thick take-off A take-off where the angle of swing is between 45 and 80 degrees.
Thin take-off A take-off where the angle of swing is greater than 80 degrees.
Three-ball break A break using three balls.
Three-ball group Three balls in contact, one of which is a yard-line ball.
Tice A ball played at the start of the game to entice the opponent to shoot at it.
Time limit The time allowed for a game or match.
Top-spin *See* forward spin.
Touch The ability to play a stroke with the correct strength.
TPO A triple peel achieved on one of the opponent's balls.
Trap A leave which will give the in-player an advantage if the out-player shoots and misses.

Treble Three balls which subtend a target angle three times that of a single ball.

Triple peel (TP) A break where a ball is peeled through its last three hoops and pegged out.

Turn A stroke or series of strokes which a player plays.

Two-ball break A break using two balls.

Upright The stanchion of a hoop.

Vertical spread A particular leave in advanced play.

Wafer cannon A cannon where there is only a wafer-thin gap between the striker's ball and the third ball.

WCF World Croquet Federation.

Windscreen wiper A pejorative term applied to shooting back and forth at a ball with bisques and missing.

Wire The upright of a hoop.

Wired A position where a ball does not have an open shot at another ball.

Wiring lift A lift conceded subject to certain conditions when a ball does not have an open shot at any other ball.

Yard-line An imaginary line one yard inside the boundaries of a court.

Yard-line area The area between the boundary and the yard-line.

Yard-line ball A ball on the yard-line.

Yard-line cannon A cannon where one of the balls is a yard-line ball.